IN THE BLINK OF AN EYE

2ND EDITION

IN THE BLINK OF AN EYE

A PERSPECTIVE ON FILM EDITING

2ND EDITION

WALTER MURCH

SILMAN-JAMES PRESS
Los Angeles

Permission was graciously extended by the respective publishers for the use of material from the following works:

The Magic Lantern by Ingmar Bergman, p. 35. © 1988 Viking Press, New York, NY, 10010. Translation by Joan Tate. Originally published as *Lanterna Magica* in 1987 by Norstedts Forlag, Sweden. Reproduced by permission of Hamish Hamilton Ltd., London.

Language in Four Dimensions by William Stokoe. New York Academy of Sciences, 1979.

Christian Science Monitor, interview with John Huston by staff writer Louise Sweeney, August 11, 1973.

Photos from the film *The Unbearable Lightness of Being* used with permission of the Saul Zaentz Co. All rights reserved. © 1988

Library of Congress Cataloging-in-Publication Data

Murch, Walter, 1943-
In the blink of an eye / by Walter Murch—2nd ed.
p. cm.
1. Motion pictures—Editing. I. Title.
TR899.M87 2001 778.5'35--dc21 2001042949
ISBN: 1-879505-62-2

42 41 40 39 38 37 36

Cover design by Heidi Frieder
Cover photographs by Michael D. Brown
Printed and bound in the United States of America

Silman-James Press

silmanjamespress.com

This is a revised transcription of a lecture on film editing given by Walter Murch in the mixing theater at Spectrum Films, Sydney, Australia, in October 1988. It was one in a series of lectures sponsored by the Australian Film Commission.

Sections of this lecture were also included in a presentation given in February 1990 to the Advanced Editing class taught by Barbara and Richard Marks as part of the UCLA Graduate School of Theater, Film, and Television.

In 1995, the main text of this book was revised and the Afterword was added. In 2001, the Afterword was rewritten to reflect current developments in digital editing.

The final chapter in this book, "Gesamtkunstkino," originally appeared in the Arts and Lesiure section of the *New York Times*, May 2, 1999.

Contents

Foreword

The thought of Walter Murch brings a smile to my face. I'm not sure exactly why. It must be the combination of his unique personality, the security inspired by his competence, and his gentleness and wisdom. Gerald MacBoingBoing grown up, still playful and enigmatic, but grounded by an immense intelligence.

Perhaps it's also because he was the essential collaborator on what are probably the best films I worked on: *The Conversation* and *The Godfather, Part II.* I have a very soft spot in my heart for those films, and *The Rain People,* because only they were the closest to the goal I had set for myself as a young man: to write original stories and screenplays only. This is something Walter always encouraged me to do, and was best achieved working with him. But Walter is a study unto himself: a philosopher and theoretician of film—a gifted director in his own right, attested to by his beautiful *Return to Oz.* Nothing is so fascinating as spending hours listening to Walter's theories of life, cinema, and the countless tidbits of wisdom that he leaves behind him like Hansel and Gretel's trail of bread: guidance and nourishment.

I smile also because we are so different from one another: Whereas I make instantaneous decisions relying on emotion and intuition only, Walter is *also* thoughtful and careful and methodical in every step he takes. Whereas I alternate between the ecstatic and despondent like Tesla's alternating current, Walter is constant and warm and reassuring. Every bit as ingenious and intuitive as I am, he is also constant.

Walter is a pioneer, as I would like to be, and the kind of person who should be listened to carefully and enjoyed. For all this, I imagine you would think that I love and respect Walter Murch very much—and I certainly do.

Francis Coppola
Napa, 1995

Preface to the Second Edition

1995 was a watershed year in film editing—it was the last time the number of films edited mechanically equaled the number of films edited digitally. Every subsequent year, the digital number has increased and the mechanical number has proportionally decreased. In 1995, no digitally edited film had yet won an Oscar for best editing. Since 1996, every winner has been edited digitally—with the notable exception of *Saving Private Ryan* in 1998.

1995 was also the year that *In the Blink of an Eye* was first published in the United States. That edition included a section on digital editing as things stood at the time. It was clear to me then that the complete digitization of the moving image was inevitable, but the time frame for that transformation was not obvious and I looked at the situation with mixed feelings. At that time I also lacked digital editing experience. (I had edited some short films on the Avid, but not an entire feature film.)

That changed the following year: I started editing *The English Patient* mechanically, but for reasons explained in this new edition of *Blink*, we changed over to digital during production. And every film that I have worked on since, including the restorations of *Touch of Evil* and *Apocalypse Now*, have been edited digitally, using the Avid Film Composer system.

It is a rule of thumb that two and a half years represent a generation in the evolution of computers. More than two of those electronic generations have passed since 1995, so I felt it was time to re-evaluate the cinematic digital landscape in general and digital editing in particular. Consequently, for this new edition of *In the Blink of an Eye*, I have completely rewritten and considerably expanded the digital editing section, including my personal experiences making the mechanical-to-digital transition and some premonitions—both technical and artistic—as we begin cinema's second century.

Walter Murch
Toronto, June 2001

Preface

Igor Stravinsky loved expressing himself and wrote a good deal on interpretation. As he bore a volcano within him, he urged restraint. Those without even the vestige of a volcano within them nodded in agreement, raised their baton, and observed restraint, while Stravinsky himself conducted his own *Apollon Musagète* as if it were Tchaikovsky. We who had read him listened and were astonished.

The Magic Lantern by Ingmar Bergman

Most of us are searching—consciously or unconsciously—for a degree of internal balance and harmony between ourselves and the outside world, and if we happen to become aware—like Stravinsky—of a volcano within us, we will compensate by urging restraint. By the same token, someone who bore a glacier within him might urge passionate abandon. The danger is, as Bergman points out, that a glacial personality in need of passionate abandon may read Stravinsky and apply restraint instead.

Many of the thoughts that follow, although presented to the public in a lecture, are therefore more truly cautionary notes to myself, working methods I have developed for coping with my own particular volcanoes and glaciers. As such, they are insights into one person's search for balance, and are perhaps interesting to others more for the glimpses of the search itself than for the specific methods that search has produced.

I would like to thank Ken Sallows for providing me with the transcription of the original lecture and the opportunity to present it to a wider audience. For cosmetic reasons, I have made certain revisions and added some footnotes to what was, for the most part, an extemporaneous dialogue between myself and the audience, whom I thank for their interest and participation. I have also updated some technical points and added an afterword that considers the impact that non-linear, digital editing has had on the process of film-making.

Special thanks also to Hilary Furlong (then of the Australian Film Commission), who was instrumental in bringing me to Australia, where the lecture was originally given.

Walter Murch
Rome, August 1995

Cuts and Shadow Cuts

It is frequently at the edges of things that we learn most about the middle: ice and steam can reveal more about the nature of water than water alone ever could. While it is true that any film worth making is going to be unique, and the conditions under which films are made are so variable that it is misleading to speak about what is "normal," *Apocalypse Now,* by almost any criteria—schedule, budget, artistic ambition, technical innovation—qualifies as the cinematic equivalent of ice and steam. Just considering the length of time it took to complete the film (I was editing picture for one year and spent another year preparing and mixing the sound), it turned out to be the longest post-production of any picture I have worked on, but that may consequently spill some light on what "normal" is, or might be.[1]

One of the reasons for that length was simply the amount of film that had been printed: 1,250,000 feet,

[1] And I had come on relatively late in the process. Richie Marks and Jerry Greenberg had already been editing for nine months when I joined them in August 1977, a few months after the end of shooting, and the three of us worked together until Jerry left in the spring of 1978. Richie and I then continued together, joined by Lisa Fruchtman, until I began to work on the soundtrack.

which works out to be just over 230 hours. Since the finished film runs just under two hours and twenty-five minutes in length, that gives a ratio of ninety-five to one. That is to say, ninety-five "unseen" minutes for every minute that found its way into the finished product. By comparison, the average ratio for theatrical features is around twenty to one.

Traveling across that ninety-five-to-one landscape was a little like forging through a thick forest, bursting upon open grassland for a while, then plunging into a forest again because there were areas, such as the helicopter sequences, where the coverage was extremely high, and other scenes where the coverage was correspondingly low. I think the Colonel Kilgore scenes alone were over 220,000 feet—and since that represents twenty-five minutes of film in the finished product, the ratio there was around one hundred to one. But many of the connecting scenes had only a master shot: Francis had used so much film and time on the big events that he compensated with minimal coverage on some of these linking scenes.

Take one of the big scenes as an example: The helicopter attack on "Charlie's Point," where Wagner's *Ride of the Valkyries* is played, was staged as an actual event and consequently filmed as a documentary rather than a series of specially composed shots. It was choreography on a vast scale of men, machines, cameras, and landscape—like some kind of diabolical toy that you could wind up and then let go. Once Francis said, "Action," the filming resembled actual combat: Eight cameras turning simultaneously (some on the ground and some in helicopters) each loaded with a thousand-foot (eleven-minute) roll of film.

At the end of one of these shots, unless there had been an obvious problem, the camera positions were changed and the whole thing was repeated. Then repeated again, and then again. They kept on going until, I guess, they felt that they had enough material, each take generating something like 8,000 feet (an hour and a half). No single take was the same as any other—very much like documentary coverage.

Anyway, at the end of it all, when the film was safely in the theaters, I sat down and figured out the total number of days that we (the editors) had worked, divided that number by the number of cuts that were in the finished product, and came up with the rate of cuts per editor per day—which turned out to be . . . 1.47!

Meaning that, if we had somehow known *exactly* where we were going at the beginning, we would have arrived there in the same number of months if each of us had made just under one-and-a-half splices per day. In other words, if I had sat down at my bench in the morning, made one cut, thought about the next cut, and gone home, then come in the next day, made the cut I thought about the day before, made another cut, and gone home, it would have taken me the same year it actually took to edit my sections of the film.

Since it takes under ten seconds to make one-and-a-half splices, the admittedly special case of *Apocalypse Now* serves to throw into exaggerated relief the fact that editing—even on a "normal" film[2]—is not so

[2] By comparison, an average theatrical feature might have a cuts-per-day figure of eight.

much a *putting together* as it is a *discovery of a path,* and that the overwhelming majority of an editor's time is not spent actually splicing film. The more film there is to work with, of course, the greater the number of pathways that can be considered, and the possibilities compound upon each other and consequently demand more time for evaluation. This is true for any film with a high shooting ratio, but in the particular case of *Apocalypse* the effect was magnified by a sensitive subject matter and a daring and unusual structure, technical innovations at every level, and the obligation felt by all concerned to do the very best work they were capable of. And perhaps most of all by the fact that this was, for Francis, a personal film, despite the large budget and the vast canvas of the subject. Regrettably few films combine such qualities and aspirations.

For every splice in the finished film there were probably fifteen "shadow" splices—splices made, considered, and then undone or lifted from the film. But even allowing for that, the remaining eleven hours and fifty-eight minutes of each working day were spent in activities that, in their various ways, served to clear and illuminate the path ahead of us: screenings, discussions, rewinding, re-screenings, meetings, scheduling, filing trims, note-taking, bookkeeping, and lots of plain deliberative thought. A vast amount of preparation, really, to arrive at the innocuously brief moment of decisive action: the cut—the moment of transition from one shot to the next—something that, appropriately enough, should look almost self-evidently simple and effortless, if it is even noticed at all.

Why Do Cuts Work?

Well, the fact is that *Apocalypse Now*, as well as every other theatrical film (except perhaps Hitchcock's *Rope*[3]), is made up of many different pieces of film joined together into a mosaic of images. The mysterious part of it, though, is that the joining of those pieces—the "cut" in American terminology[4]—actually does seem to work, even though it represents a total and instantaneous displacement of one field of vision with another, a displacement that sometimes also entails a jump forward or backward in time as well as space.

It works; but it could easily have been otherwise, since nothing in our day-to-day experience seems to prepare us for such a thing. Instead, from the moment we get up in the morning until we close our eyes at night, the visual reality we perceive is a continuous

[3] A film composed of only ten shots, each ten minutes long, invisibly joined together, so that the impression is of a complete lack of editing.

[4] I was aware, talking to an Australian audience, of the bias inherent in our respective languages. In the States, film is "cut," which puts the emphasis on *separation*. In Australia (and in Great Britain), film is "joined," with the emphasis on *bringing together*.

stream of linked images: In fact, for millions of years—tens, hundreds of millions of years—life on Earth has experienced the world this way. Then suddenly, at the beginning of the twentieth century, human beings were confronted with something else—edited film.

Under these circumstances, it wouldn't have been at all surprising to find that our brains had been "wired" by evolution and experience to reject film editing. If that had been the case, then the single-shot movies of the Lumière Brothers—or films like Hitchcock's *Rope*—would have become the standard. For a number of practical (as well as artistic) reasons, it is good that it did not.

The truth of the matter is that film is actually being "cut" twenty-four times a second. Each frame is a displacement from the previous one—it is just that in a continuous shot, the space/time displacement from frame to frame is small enough (twenty milliseconds) for the audience to see it as *motion within a context* rather than as twenty-four different contexts a second. On the other hand, when the visual displacement is great enough (as at the moment of the cut), we are forced to re-evaluate the new image as a *different context*: miraculously, most of the time we have no problem in doing this.

What we *do* seem to have difficulty accepting are the kind of displacements that are neither subtle nor total: Cutting from a full-figure master shot, for instance, to a slightly tighter shot that frames the actors from the ankles up. The new shot in this case is different enough to signal that *something* has changed, but not different enough to make us re-evaluate its context: The displacement of the image is neither motion nor change of context, and the collision of these two ideas produces a mental jarring—a jump—that is comparatively disturbing.[5]

At any rate, the discovery early in this century that certain kinds of cutting "worked" led almost immediately to the discovery that films could be shot discontinuously, which was the cinematic equivalent of the discovery of flight: In a practical sense, films were no longer "earthbound" in time and space. If we could make films only by assembling all the elements simultaneously, as in the theater, the range of possible subjects would be comparatively narrow. Instead, Discontinuity is King: It is the central fact during the production phase of filmmaking, and almost all decisions are directly related to it in one way or another—how to overcome its difficulties and/or how to best take advantage of its strengths.[6]

The other consideration is that even if everything *were* available simultaneously, it is just very difficult

---

[5] A beehive can apparently be moved two inches each night without disorienting the bees the next morning. Surprisingly, if it is moved two *miles,* the bees also have no problem: They are forced by the total displacement of their environment to re-orient their sense of direction, which they can do easily enough. But if the hive is moved two *yards,* the bees will become fatally confused. The environment does not seem different to them, so they do not re-orient themselves, and as a result, they will not recognize their own hive when they return from foraging, hovering instead in the empty space where the hive used to be, while the hive itself sits just two yards away.

[6] When Stanley Kubrick was directing *The Shining,* he wanted to shoot the film in continuity and to have all sets and actors available all the time. He took over almost the entire studio at Elstree (London), built all the sets simultaneously, and they sat there, pre-lit, for however long it took him to shoot the film. But *The Shining* remains a special exception to the general rule of discontinuity.

to shoot long, continuous takes and have all the contributing elements work each time. European filmmakers tend to shoot more complex master shots than the Americans, but even if you are Ingmar Bergman, there's a limit to what you can handle: Right at the end, some special effect might not work or someone might forget their lines or some lamp might blow a fuse, and now the whole thing has to be done again. The longer the take, of course, the greater the chances of a mistake.

So there is a considerable logistical problem of getting everything together at the same time, and then just as serious a problem in getting it all to "work" every time. The result is that, for practical reasons alone, we don't follow the pattern of the Lumière Brothers or of *Rope.*

On the other hand, apart from matters of convenience, discontinuity also allows us to choose the best camera angle for each emotion and story point, which we can edit together for a cumulatively greater impact. If we were limited to a continuous stream of images, this would be difficult, and films would not be as sharp and to the point as they are.[7]

[7] Visual discontinuity—although not in the temporal sense—is the most striking feature of Ancient Egyptian painting. Each part of the human body was represented by its most characteristic and revealing angle: head in profile, shoulders frontal, arms and legs in profile, torso frontal—and then all these different angles were combined in one figure. To us today, with our preference for the unifying laws of perspective, this gives an almost comic "twisted" look to the people of Ancient Egypt—but it may be that in some remote future, our films, with their combination of many different angles (each being the most "revealing" for its particular subject), will look just as comic and twisted.

And yet, beyond even these considerations, cutting is more than just the convenient means by which discontinuity is rendered continuous. It is in *and for itself*—by the very force of its paradoxical suddenness—a positive influence in the creation of a film. We would want to cut even if discontinuity were not of such great practical value.

So the central fact of all this is that cuts *do work*. But the question still remains: *Why?* It is kind of like the bumble-bee, which should not be able to fly, but does.

We will get back to this mystery in a few moments.

"Cut Out the Bad Bits"

Many years ago, my wife, Aggie, and I went back to England for our first anniversary (she is English, although we'd been married in the United States), and I met some of her childhood friends for the first time.

"Well, what is it that you do?" one of them asked, and I replied that I was studying film editing. "Oh, editing," he said, "that's where you cut out the bad bits." Of course, I became (politely) incensed: "It is much more than that. Editing is structure, color, dynamics, manipulation of time, all of these other things, etc., etc." What he had in mind was home movies: "Oop, there's a bad bit, cut it out and paste the rest back together." Actually, twenty-five years down the road, I've come to respect his unwitting wisdom.

Because, in a certain sense, editing *is* cutting out the bad bits, the tough question is, *What makes a bad bit?* When you are shooting a home movie and the camera wanders, that's obviously a bad bit, and it's clear that you want to cut it out. The goal of a home movie is usually pretty simple: an unrestructured record of events in continuous time. The goal of narrative films is much more complicated because of the fragmented time structure and the need to indicate internal states of being, and so it becomes proportionately more complicated to identify what is a "bad bit." And what is bad in one film may be good in another. In fact, one way of looking at the process of making a film is to think of it as the search to identify what—for the particular film you are working on—is a uniquely "bad bit." So, the editor embarks on the search to identify these "bad bits" and cut them out, provided that doing so does not disrupt the structure of the "good bits" that are left.

Which leads me to chimpanzees.

About forty years ago, after the double-helix structure of DNA was discovered, biologists hoped that they now had a kind of map of the genetic architecture of each organism. Of course, they didn't expect the structure of the DNA to look like the organism they were studying (the way a map of England *looks* like England), but rather that each point in the organism would somehow correspond to an equivalent point in the DNA.

That's not what they found, though. For instance, when they began to compare them closely, they were surprised to discover that the DNA for the human and the chimpanzee were surprisingly similar. So much so—ninety-nine percent identical—as to be inadequate to explain all of the obvious differences between us.

So where do the differences come from?

Biologists were eventually forced to realize that there must be something else—still under much discussion—that controlled the *order* in which the various pieces of information stored in the DNA would be activated and the *rates* at which that information would be activated as the organism grew.

In the early stages of fetal development, it is difficult to tell the difference between human and chimp embryos. And yet, as they grow, they reach a point where differences become apparent, and from that point on, the differences become more and more obvious. For instance, the choice of what comes first, the brain or the skull. In human beings, the priority is brain first, skull next, because the emphasis is on maximizing the size of the brain. Any time you look at a newborn human infant you can see that the skull is not yet fully closed around the top of the still-growing brain.

With chimpanzees, the priority is reversed: skull first, *then* brain—probably for reasons that have to do with the harsher environment into which the chimp is born. The command from the chimp's sequence is, "Fill up this empty space with as much brain as you can." But there's only so much brain you can get in there before you can't fill it up anymore. At any rate, it seems to be more important for a chimp to be born with a hard head than a big brain. There's a similar interplay between an endless list of things: The thumb and the fingers, skeletal posture, certain bones being fully formed before certain muscular developments, etc.

My point is that the information in the DNA can be seen as uncut film and the mysterious sequencing code as the editor. You could sit in one room with a pile of dailies and another editor could sit in the next room with exactly the same footage and both of you would make different films out of the same material. Each is going to make different choices about how to structure it, which is to say *when* and *in what order* to release those various pieces of information.

Do we know, for instance, that the gun is loaded *before* Madame X gets into her car, or is that something we only learn *after* she is in the car? Either choice creates a different sense of the scene. And so you proceed, piling one difference on top of another. Reversing the comparison, you can look at the human and the chimp as different films edited from the same set of dailies.[8]

I'm not assigning relative values here to a chimpanzee or a human being. Let's just say that each is appropriate to the environment in which it belongs: I would be wrong swinging from a branch in the middle of the jungle, and a chimpanzee would be wrong writing this book. The point is not their intrinsic value, but rather the inadvisability of changing one's mind in the process of creating one of them. Don't start making a chimpanzee and then decide to turn it into a human being instead. That produces a stitched-together Frankenstein's monster, and we've all seen its equivalent in the theaters: Film "X" would have been a nice little movie, perfectly suited to its "environment," but in the middle of production someone got an inflated idea about its possibilities, and, as a result, it became boring and pretentious. It was

[8] By the same token, a chimpanzee and a cockroach are made from different "dailies" to begin with.

a chimpanzee film that someone tried to turn it into a human-being film, and it came out being neither.

Or film "Y," which was an ambitious project that tried to deal with complex, subtle issues, but the studio got to it and ordered additional material to be shot, filled with action and sex, and, as a result, a great potential was reduced to something less, neither human nor chimp.

Most with the Least

You can never judge the quality of a sound mix simply by counting the number of tracks it took to produce it. Terrible mixes have been produced from a hundred tracks. By the same token, wonderful mixes have been made from only three tracks. It depends on the initial choices that were made, the quality of the sounds, and how capable the blend of those sounds was of exciting emotions hidden in the hearts of the audience. The underlying principle: Always try to do the most with the least—with the emphasis on try. You may not always succeed, but *attempt* to produce the greatest effect in the viewer's mind by the least number of things on screen. Why? Because you want to do only what is necessary to engage the imagination of the audience—suggestion is always more effective than exposition. Past a certain point, the more effort you put into wealth of detail, the more you encourage the audience to become spectators rather than participants. The same principle applies to all the various crafts of filmmaking: acting, art direction, photography, music, costume, etc.

And, of course, it applies to editing as well. You would never say that a certain film was well-edited because it had more cuts in it. Frequently, it takes more work and discernment to decide where *not* to cut—don't feel you have to cut just because you are being paid to. You are being paid to make decisions, and as far as whether to cut or not, the editor is actually making twenty-four decisions a second: "No. No. No. No. No. No. No. No. No. No. Yes!"

An overactive editor, who changes shots too frequently, is like a tour guide who can't stop pointing things out: "And up there we have the Sistine Ceiling, and over here we have the Mona Lisa, and, by the way, look at these floor tiles . . ." If you are on a tour, you do want the guide to point things out for you, of course, but some of the time you just want to walk around and see what *you* see. If the guide—that is to say, the editor—doesn't have the confidence to let people themselves occasionally choose what they want to look at, or to leave things to their imagination, then he is pursuing a goal (complete control) that in the end is self-defeating. People will eventually feel constrained and then resentful from the constant pressure of his hand on the backs of their necks.

Well, if what I'm saying is to do more with less, then is there any way to say how much less? Is it possible to take this right to its absurd logical conclusion and say, "Don't cut at all?" Now we've come back to our first problem: Film is cut for practical reasons *and* film is cut because cutting—that sudden disruption of reality—can be an effective tool in itself. So, if the goal is as few cuts as possible, when you *have* to make a cut, what is it that makes it a good one?

The Rule of Six

The first thing discussed in film-school editing classes is what I'm going to call three-dimensional continuity: In shot A, a man opens a door, walks halfway across the room, and then the film cuts to the next shot, B, picking him up at that same halfway point and continuing with him the rest of the way across the room, where he sits down at his desk, or something.

For many years, particularly in the early years of sound film, that was the rule. You struggled to preserve continuity of three-dimensional space, and it was seen as a failure of rigor or skill to violate it.[9] Jumping people around in space was just not done, except, perhaps, in extreme circumstances—fights or earthquakes—where there was a lot of violent action going on.

I actually place this three-dimensional continuity at the bottom of a list of six *criteria* for what makes a

---

[9] The problem with this thinking can be seen in any multi-camera situation-comedy on television. Because the cameras are filming simultaneously, the actors are necessarily always "correct" as far as their spatial continuity and relation to each other is concerned, but that absolutely does not prevent bad cuts from being made all the time.

good cut. At the top of the list is Emotion, the thing you come to last, if at all, at film school largely because it's the hardest thing to define and deal with. *How do you want the audience to feel?* If they are feeling what you want them to feel all the way through the film, you've done about as much as you can ever do. What they finally remember is not the editing, not the camerawork, not the performances, not even the story—it's how they felt.

An ideal cut (for me) is the one that satisfies all the following six criteria at once: 1) it is true to the emotion of the moment; 2) it advances the story; 3) it occurs at a moment that is rhythmically interesting and "right"; 4) it acknowledges what you might call "eye-trace"—the concern with the location and movement of the audience's focus of interest within the frame; 5) it respects "planarity"—the grammar of three dimensions transposed by photography to two (the questions of stage-line, etc.); 6) and it respects the three-dimensional continuity of the actual space (where people are in the room and in relation to one another).

1) Emotion	51%
2) Story	23%
3) Rhythm	10%
4) Eye-trace	7%
5) Two-dimensional plane of screen	5%
6) Three-dimensional space of action	4%

Emotion, at the top of the list, is the thing that you should try to preserve at all costs. If you find you have to sacrifice certain of those six things to make a cut, sacrifice your way up, item by item, from the bottom.

For instance, if you are considering a range of possible edits for a particular moment in the film, and you find that there is one cut that gives the right emotion *and* moves the story forward, *and* is rhythmically satisfying, *and* respects eye-trace and planarity, *but* it fails to preserve the continuity of three-dimensional space, then, by all means, that is the cut you should make. If none of the other edits has the right emotion, then sacrificing spatial continuity is well worth it.

The values I put after each item are slightly tongue-in-cheek, but not completely: Notice that the top two on the list (emotion and story) are worth far more than the bottom four (rhythm, eye-trace, planarity, spatial continuity), and when you come right down to it, under most circumstances, the top of the list—emotion—is worth more than all five of the things underneath it.

And, in fact, there is a practical side to this, which is that if the emotion is right and the story is advanced in a unique, interesting way, in the right rhythm, the audience will tend to be unaware of (or unconcerned about) editorial problems with lower-order items like eye-trace, stage-line, spatial continuity, etc. The general principle seems to be that satisfying the criteria of items higher on the list tends to obscure problems with items lower on the list, but not vice-versa: For instance, getting Number 4 (eye-trace) working properly will minimize a problem with Number 5 (stage-line), whereas if Number 5 (stage-line) is correct but

Number 4 (eye-trace) is not taken into consideration, the cut will be unsuccessful.

Now, in practice, you will find that those top three things on the list—emotion, story, rhythm—are extremely tightly connected. The forces that bind them together are like the bonds between the protons and neutrons in the nucleus of the atom. Those are, by far, the tightest bonds, and the forces connecting the lower three grow progressively weaker as you go down the list.

Most of the time you will be able to satisfy all six criteria: the three-dimensional space and the two-dimensional plane of the screen and the eye-trace, and the rhythm and story and emotion will all fall into place. And, of course, you should always aim for this, if possible—never accept less when more is available to you.

What I'm suggesting is a list of priorities. If you have to give up something, don't ever give up emotion before story. Don't give up story before rhythm, don't give up rhythm before eye-trace, don't give up eye-trace before planarity, and don't give up planarity before spatial continuity.

Misdirection

Underlying these considerations is the central preoccupation of a film editor, which should be to put himself/herself in place of the audience. What is the audience going to be thinking at any particular moment? Where are they going to be looking? What do you want them to think about? What do they need to think about? And, of course, what do you want them to feel? If you keep this in mind (and it's the preoccupation of every magician), then you are a kind of magician. Not in the supernatural sense, just an everyday, working magician.

Houdini's job was to create a sense of wonder, and to do that he didn't want you to look *here* (to the right) because that's where he was undoing his chains, so he found a way to make you look *there* (to the left). He was "misdirecting" you, as magicians say. He was doing something that would cause ninety-nine percent of you to look over here when he wanted you to. And an editor can do that and does do that—and *should* do that.

Sometimes, though, you can get caught up in the details and lose track of the overview. When that happens to me, it is usually because I have been looking at the image as the miniature it is in the editing room, rather than seeing it as the mural that it will become when projected in a theater. Something that will quickly restore the correct perspective is to imagine yourself very small, and the screen very large, and pretend that you are watching the finished film in a thousand-seat theater filled with people, and that the film is beyond the possibility of any further changes. If you still like what you see, it is probably okay. If not, you will now most likely have a better idea of how to correct the problem, whatever it is. One of the tricks I use to help me achieve this perspective is to cut out little paper dolls—a man and a woman—and put one on each side of the editing screen: The size of the dolls (a few inches high) is proportionately correct to make the screen seem as if it is thirty feet wide.

Seeing Around the Edge of the Frame

The film editor is one of the few people working on the production of a film who does not know the exact conditions under which it was shot (or has the *ability* not to know) *and* who can at the same time have a tremendous influence on the film.

If you have been on and around the set most of the time, as the actors, the producer, director, cameraman, art director, etc., have been, you can get caught up in the sometimes bloody practicalities of gestation and delivery. And then when you see the dailies, you can't help, in your mind's eye, seeing around the edge of the frame—you can imagine everything that was there, physically and emotionally, just beyond what was actually photographed.

"We worked like hell to get that shot, it has to be in the film." You (the director, in this case) are convinced that what you got was what you wanted, but there's a possibility that you may to forcing yourself to see it that way because it cost so much—in money, time, angst—to get it.

By the same token, there are occasions when you shoot something that you dislike, when everyone is in a bad mood, and you say under protest: "All right, I'll do this, we'll get this one close-up, and then it's a wrap." Later on, when you look at that take, all you can remember was the hateful moment it was shot, and so you may be blind to the potentials it might have in a different context.

The editor, on the other hand, should try to see only what's on the screen, as the audience will. Only in this way can the images be freed from the context of their creation. By focusing on the screen, the editor will, hopefully, use the moments that should be used, even if they may have been shot under duress, and reject moments that should be rejected, even though they cost a terrible amount of money and pain.

I guess I'm urging the preservation of a certain kind of virginity. Don't *unnecessarily* allow yourself to be impregnated by the conditions of shooting. Try to keep up with what's going on but try to have as little specific knowledge of it as possible because, ultimately, the audience knows nothing about any of this—and you are the ombudsman for the audience.

The director, of course, is the person most familiar with all of the things that went on during the shoot, so he is the most burdened with this surplus, beyond-the-frame information. Between the end of shooting and before the first cut is finished, the very best thing that can happen to the director (and the film) is that he say goodbye to everyone and disappear for two weeks—up to the mountains or down to the sea or out to Mars or somewhere—and try to discharge this surplus.

Wherever he goes, he should try to think, as much as possible, about things that have absolutely nothing to do with the film. It is difficult, but it is necessary to create a barrier, a cellular wall between shooting and editing. Fred Zinnemann would go climbing in the Alps after the end of shooting, just to put himself in a potentially life-threatening situation where he had to be *there*, not day-dreaming about the film's problems.

Then, after a few weeks, he would come down from the Alps, back to earth; he would sit down in a dark room, alone, the arc light would ignite, and he would watch his film. He would still be, inherently, brimming with those images from beyond the edge of the frame (a director will never be fully able to forget them), but if he had gone straight from shooting to editing, the confusion would be worse and he would have gotten the two different thought processes of shooting and editing irrevocably mixed up.

Do everything you can to help the director erect this barrier for himself so that when he first sees the film, he can say, "All right, I'm going to pretend that I had nothing to do with this film. It needs some work. What needs to be done?"

And so you try as hard as you can to separate out what you wish from what is actually there, never abandoning your ultimate dreams for the film, but trying as hard as you can to see what is actually on the screen.

Dreaming in Pairs

In many ways, the film editor performs the same role for the director as the text editor does for the writer of a book—to encourage certain courses of action, to counsel against others, to discuss whether to include specific material in the finished work or whether new material needs to be added. At the end of the day, though, it is the writer who then goes off and puts the words together.

But in film, the editor also has the responsibility for actually assembling the images (that is to say, the "words") in a certain order and in a certain rhythm. And here it becomes the *director's* role to offer advice and counsel much as he would to an actor interpreting a part. So it seems that the film editor/director relationship oscillates back and forth during the course of the project, the numerator becoming the denominator and vice versa.

In dream therapy there is a technique that pairs the patient—the *dreamer*, in this case—with someone who is there to *listen* to the dream. As soon as possible after waking, the dreamer gets together with his listener to review the dreams of the previous night.

Frequently there is nothing, or just a single disappointing image, but this is usually enough to begin the process. Once the image is described, the listener's job is to propose an imaginary sequence of events based on that fragment. An airplane, for instance, is all that is remembered. The listener immediately proposes that it must have been an airliner flying over Tahiti filled with golf balls for a tournament in Indonesia. No sooner has this description been offered than the dreamer finds himself protesting: "No, it was a bi-plane, flying over the battlefields of France, and Hannibal was shooting arrows at it from his legion of elephants." In other words, the dream itself, hidden in the memory, rises to its own defense when it hears itself being challenged by an alternate version, and so reveals itself. This revelation about bi-planes and elephants can in turn prompt the listener to elaborate another improvisation, which will coax out another aspect of the hidden dream, and so on, until as much of the dream is revealed as possible.

The relationship between director and editor is somewhat similar in that the director is generally the dreamer and the editor is the listener. But even for the most well-prepared of directors, there are limits to the imagination and memory, particularly at the level of fine detail, and so it is the editor's job to propose alternate scenarios as bait to encourage the sleeping dream to rise to its defense and thus reveal itself more fully. And these scenarios unfold themselves at the largest level (should such-and-such a scene be removed from the film for the good of the whole?) and at the most detailed (should this shot end on this frame or 1/24th of a second later on the *next* frame?). But sometimes it is the editor who is the dreamer and the director who is the listener, and it is he who now offers the bait to tempt the collective dream to reveal more of itself.

As any fisherman can tell you, it is the quality of the bait that determines the kind of fish you catch.

Team Work: Multiple Editors

Not only does the editor collaborate with the director, there are frequent times when two or more editors are working simultaneously, sometimes with equal authority. This seems odd to many people, who do not see the same thing happening with directors of photography or production designers. But for some reason, which has to do with the collaborative mentality of editors and with the fact that the time pressure of post-production is not quite so unforgiving in its consequences as it is during production, multiple editors are often employed. I have worked, and enjoyed, collaborating with other editors on many films: *The Conversation, Apocalypse Now, The Unbearable Lightness of Being,* and *Godfather, Part III.*

The main advantage to collaborative editing is speed; the main risk is lack of coherence. But if there are upward of 350,000 feet of workprint (sixty-five hours), you are probably going to need to take that risk and have two editors, or at least an associate editor working under supervision. But problems can sometimes arise if there is just one editor on a film and he develops a locked viewpoint about the material. This is particularly troublesome if the director and the editor have not worked together before and have no time to develop a common language. In this case, it might not be a bad idea to consider having multiple editors.

The Godfather was the first film on which Francis worked with two editors. Originally there had been just a single editor, but the problem of locked viewpoint became acute and he was let go after several months. The decision was made to reconstitute what had been done up to that point and start again, but because they had effectively lost those months, and it looked as though the film was going to be almost three hours long with an inflexible deadline, it made sense to hire two editors. The film was still shooting and there was just a lot of work to do: Each editor had a ninety-minute film to complete in twenty-four weeks. But unlike the later *Godfather, Part II* or *Apocalypse*, the work was split strictly in half. Bill Reynolds cut the first part and Peter Zinner cut the last part. There's a specific point where Bill's section ends and Peter's begins.

On *Godfather, Part II*, although the responsibility for editing was divided up in a checkerboard pattern, scenes were initially cut and recut by the same person.[10] But when Francis began to play with the structure of the film, people found themselves recutting what others had originally edited.

[10] The editors of *Godfather, Part II,* were Peter Zinner, Barry Malkin, and Richard Marks.

The interest on a $25 million film is around $250,000 a month. If having two editors can help you release that film a month earlier, they will have repaid a good portion, if not all, of their salaries for the whole film. It is simply a matter of how much you want to achieve in the time you have available. If you end up with a cut-per-day rate of 1.47, as we did on *Apocalypse*, that means that many different avenues have been explored to get to the final product. If that's what you want to do, you probably need more than one editor.

The Decisive Moment

While Phil Kaufman was shooting *The Unbearable Lightness of Being* in France, I was editing it in Berkeley, California—6,000 miles away. The dailies would be shipped approximately every two weeks, and I would then sit and watch ten hours or so of film, taking notes, making sure it was in sync, getting ready to code it, etc.

But in addition to the usual procedures, I also would select at least one representative frame from every setup (camera position) and take a still photograph of it off the workprint. We then had these photos developed and printed at the local "one hour" place, like family snapshots, and they were put onto panels arranged according to scene. Whenever a setup had complex staging or a moving camera, it was necessary to take more than one photo (I think the most that I ever took for *Unbearable* was seven, which was for a very complicated party scene)—usually it was three, and most of the time it was just one.

We had to use a special reproducing negative to make these pictures, since an ordinary snapshot negative produces too much contrast. The speed of the film is low—about ASA 2 or something—so the time exposure has to be quite long, but it worked out well: The photos were actually pretty close approximations of the real color balance and contrast ratio of the film.

The photographs are a great help in later discussions with the director about what was shot and how it was shot—they resolve those kinds of discussions very quickly.

They also provide a record of some details beyond the ability of even the best continuity person: The particulars of an actor's hairline, or a little peculiarity of costume, the way the collar flips up or down, or how rosy somebody's complexion was, or whether their hat left a mark on their forehead when they took it off—those kinds of things.

They are also a great resource for the publicity department or anyone else coming onto the film at a later date. You can instantly see and cross-reference characters in all kinds of different emotional states, as well as the photography, the costumes, and the scenery.

Also, just because of the way they were displayed, the pictures tended to collide against each other in interesting ways. On *Unbearable*, we had perhaps sixteen panels of photos, 130 photos to a panel, and each panel was laid out like a page of a book: You "read" the photos from left to right and then down a row, left to right again, etc., just like reading text, and when you got to the bottom of one panel, you went up to the top of the next and read

PRAKTICA
620
2·2

Two frames of Teresa (played by Juliette Binoche) from *The Unbearable Lightness of Being*. The three-digit numbers in the lower left-hand corner of each picture (620, 296) refer to the setup number of the shot from which the frame was taken, and the number (2.2) in the adjacent rectangle of #620 identifies that frame as occupying a certain place in the sequence—frame two in a series of two.

621
4.4

Two frames of Sabina (played by Lena Olin) from *The Unbearable Lightness of Being*. The numbering system here is the same as for Teresa's photos on the previous pages. Both these frames come from the impromptu photo session between Sabina and Teresa.

542

Two frames of Teresa from *The Unbearable Lightness of Being*. In the case of #542, one frame was sufficient to give a complete idea of the setup. Number 635, however, required three photos—of which this is number two—because of the complex nature of the shot. This comes from the same scene as #634 of Sabina and the two shots were cut together in the finished film.

across the first line, etc. So the juncture *between* those panels was an interesting thing to look at, because it juxtaposed frames that were never meant to go together and yet there they were, right next to each other. And sometimes you got sparks out of that, it would cause you to think about things, editorial leaps, that otherwise you might never have thought of without this system.

But the most interesting asset of the photos for me was that they provided the hieroglyphs for a language of emotions.

What word expresses the concept of ironic anger tinged with melancholy? There isn't a word for it, in English anyway, but you can see that specific emotion represented in this photograph.

Or the photo may represent a kind of nervous anticipation: The character is scared and lustful at the same time, and yet she is confused because that lust is for another woman. And that woman is sleeping with her husband. So what does that mean?

Whatever it means, it is there in her expression, in the angle of her head and her hair and her neck and the tension in the muscles and the set of her mouth and what is in her eyes. And if you can simply point to an expression on an actor's face, you have a way around some of the difficulties of language in dealing with the subtleties of nameless emotions. You, as the director, can say, "That's what I want. The sequence we are working on should have more of that, you know. I want it to embody the nameless but familiar emotion I see in that photograph."

The editor's job now is to choose the right images and make those images follow one another at the right rate to express something like what is captured in that photograph.

In choosing a representative frame, what you're looking for is an image that distills the essence of the thousands of frames that make up the shot in question, what Cartier-Bresson—referring to still photography—called the "decisive moment." So I think, more often than not, the image that I chose wound up in the film. And also, more often than not, quite close to the cut point.

When you look at dailies, there's a pitfall similar to the one that you may fall into during casting sessions. For the actor who is walking through the door, this casting session is the one and only time that he is going to present him or herself to you. This is a tremendously important moment for him, but for you, this may be the sixtieth person you've seen that day. Inevitably there is a kind of mental glaze that may form after a while that stops you thinking as sharply as you should.

Well, dailies are like that, too. Each shot is auditioning for your approval. Take five: "How about me? I can do this." Then take seven comes in the door: "How about this?" Take nine: "Or this?"

And to keep your awareness, to really be alive to the possibilities in each shot, you have to keep jabbing yourself. You try to remain fresh and see the wonderful things and make records of those as well as the things that may not be so wonderful. Which is what you have to do when you are casting a film.

But if you have to choose a representative set of stills from every setup, you will automatically start thinking differently—you have to be analytical right from the beginning, which is what you should be when you are looking at dailies. But, everyone being human and dailies sometimes going on as long as they do, we sometimes tend to just sit there and let the dailies roll over us. What this photo system does is just tip you up out of your chair a bit. It is an encouragement to do what you should be doing anyway. And it is the beginning of the editorial process. You are already beginning to edit at the point that you say, "I like this frame rather than that frame."

Methods and Machines: Marble and Clay

The tools you choose to edit with can have a determining effect on the final product. But when I started editing in 1965, there was really just one option, at least in Hollywood: the Moviola, a "standup" editing machine—virtually unchanged since the 1930s—that looks something like a sewing machine (and sounds like one). In the early days of Zoetrope Studios, which was founded on a European model, we used imported Steenbecks or KEMs, "horizontal" editing machines from Germany that were quieter and handled the film more gently, had two large screens and two sound tracks, and were better able to handle large amounts of film. Now, of course, the landscape has been permanently altered by the computer—electronic digital editing machines, such as Avid and Lightworks, that harness together a video display terminal and a computer with a large-scale memory bank where the film's images and sounds can be stored digitally.[11]

[11] For a more complete survey of the current non-linear systems, see the Afterword: Non-Linear, Digital Editing—The Unbearable Lightness.

I feel equally comfortable working on a Moviola, a KEM Universal, or an Avid. It depends on the film, the film's budget and schedule, and on my hunch about the style of the director and how long the average take is going to be. *The Conversation* was edited on a KEM, *Julia* on a Moviola, *Apocalypse Now* on a KEM, whereas I used both on *Unbearable*—it started out on a Moviola and changed to a KEM. With the KEM, I arrange things opposite of the way they are normally done, so that the screen directly in front of me is my search screen and the soundtrack in front of me is in sync with that. The screen on the left side and the sound on the right side are in sync with each other and hold the assembled film. If I were working on a bench, that would be what's going through the synchronizer.

In fact, speaking of benches, I should add that I work standing up: My KEM is raised about fifteen inches off the floor to put it at the right height for me. One of the things I always liked about the Moviola is that you stand up to work, holding the Moviola in a kind of embrace—dancing with it, in a way—so it was frustrating for me to have to sit down at the KEM. I edited both *The Conversation* and *Apocalypse* that way, sitting down, but a voice in the back of my head kept telling me something wasn't quite right. And so when I came to edit *Unbearable,* I had the KEM raised up on two plywood boxes.

Editing is a kind of surgery—and have you ever seen a surgeon sitting to perform an operation? Editing is also like cooking—and no one sits down at the stove to cook. But most of all, editing is a kind of dance—the finished film is a kind of crystallized dance—and when have you ever seen a dancer sitting down to dance?

Other than the "standing/sitting" question, the differences between the Moviola system and the KEM system boil down to sculptural ones: The Moviola system "emulsifies" the film into little bits (individual shots) and then the editor reassembles it out of those bits, like making something out of clay. You take a little bit of clay and you stick it here and you take another little bit of clay and you stick it *there.* At the beginning of the process there is nothing in front of you, then there is something in front of you, and then there is finally the finished thing all built up out of little clay bricks, little pellets of information.

With the KEM system, I don't ever break the film down into individual shots—I leave it in ten-minute rolls in the order in which it came from the lab. In sculptural terms, this is like a block of marble—the sculpture is already there, hidden within the stone, and you reveal it by taking away, rather than building it up piece by piece from nothing, as you do with clay. It is really the difference between "random-access" editing and its opposite, whatever that is called—"linear-access," let's say.

Computerized digital editing and, strangely enough, good old-fashioned Moviola editing with an assistant, are both random-access, non-linear systems: You ask for something specific and that thing—that thing alone—is delivered to you as quickly as possible. You are only shown what you ask for. The Avid is faster at it than the Moviola, but the process is the same.

That's a drawback for me because your choices can then only be as good as your requests, and sometimes that is not enough. There is a higher level that comes through *recognition*: You may not be able to articulate what you want, but you can recognize it when you see it.

What do I mean by that? Well, if you learn to speak a foreign language, you will find that there is a gap between how well you can speak it and how well you can understand it when it is spoken to you. A human being's ability to understand a foreign language is always greater than his ability to speak it.

And when you make a film, you are trying to learn a foreign language—it just happens to be a unique language that is only spoken by this one film. If you have to articulate everything, as you do with a random-access system like video/computer or Moviola/assistant, you are limited by what and how much you can articulate and how good your original notes were. Whereas the advantage of the KEM's linear system is that I do not always have to be speaking to it—there are times when *it* speaks to *me*. The system is constantly presenting things for consideration, and a sort of dialogue takes place. I might say, "I want to see that close-up of Teresa, number 317, in roll 45." But I'll put that roll on the machine, and as I spool down to number 317 (which may be hundreds of feet from the start), the machine shows me everything at high speed down to that point, saying in effect: "How about this instead? Or this?" And I find, more often than not, long before I get down to shot 317, that I've had three other ideas triggered by the material that I have seen flashing by me.

"Oh, this other shot is much better than the one I thought I wanted." As soon as I saw it, I recognized it as a possibility, whereas I couldn't articulate it as a choice.

When you look at dailies the first time, you have a relatively fixed idea—based on the script—of what you are looking for. Later on, though, you review some of your original notes, and they will say, for instance: "212-4: NG." What does that mean? It meant that *at the time* you thought take four of Slate 212 was No Good, and you didn't bother to make a note of why you thought so. Well, many times in the re-editing, what you thought was originally unusable may come to be your salvation.

If it was a question of only one shot, or two dozen shots, you could probably deal with the problem of second-guessing those original notes, but, in fact, an ordinary film will have 700, 1,000, 2,000 setups with more than two printed takes per setup on average, and so there may easily be two to four thousand shots that you have to have an opinion about. That's a lot of second-guessing, so you tend to fall back on your first impressions in the original notes. Which are valuable, but limited, if that is all you have.

Whereas with the KEM system, because the film is all stored in these big rolls in an *almost* arbitrary way, you are learning something new about the material as you search for what you think you want. You are actually doing creative work, and you may find what you *really* want rather than what you *thought* you wanted. This system is useful enough in the original assembly of the scene, in helping you to familiarize yourself with the material, but it becomes particularly valuable in the recutting, where your original notes—heavily influenced by the script—become less and less useful as the film finds its own voice.

There are limits, of course: A system that is too linear (which means that you have to spend too much time searching before you find what you want) would be burdensome. You would quickly become overwhelmed and/or bored with it. So there is a golden mean somewhere. If the system is completely random-access, that is a defect, in my opinion. But if it is too linear, that's a defect as well. What I've found, personally, is that given the attitude I have toward the material, given the speed that I work, and given the mechanical speed of the KEM itself, keeping the dailies in ten-minute reels in shooting order adds just about the right amount of chaos that I need in order to work the way I want to.

The digital systems, Avid and Lightworks, are promising because they offer the potential to merge the best of the Moviola's non-linear approach with the best of the KEM's ability to handle and review large amounts of material quickly. At this point, there is still some procedural awkwardness with the digital systems, but I expect those to be smoothed out over time.

In any case, there are certain things that remain the same for me no matter what system I am using. I would always review the material twice: once at the beginning, the day after the material was shot, noting down my first impressions and including any notes the director cares to give me. And then when I was ready to cut a particular scene, I would collect all the relevant material and review it again, making notes in more detail than the first time.

When you look at rushes the second time, you have evolved and the film has evolved. You will see different things than you saw the first time, because you may have assembled scenes that hadn't been shot the first time you saw the material, and strengths or problems may be emerging with characters and events as they unfold.

In an ideal world, what I would like to do is assemble a first cut and then stop and just look at all the dailies again, fresh. Whether I would ever actually be able to do that is another question: The present schedule of films, at any rate, prohibits such a thing. This is where the hidden virtues of the linear (KEM) system come in—because of the way the material is stored, in ten-minute rolls of film, it is constantly being reviewed. If this were gardening, I would be talking about the virtues of turning over the soil and aerating it.

In the actual editing of a scene, I will keep on working until I can no longer "see myself" in the material. When I review my first assembly of a scene, more often than not I can still vividly (too vividly!) recall making the decisions that led to each of the cuts. But as the scene is reworked and refined, it reaches a point, hopefully, where the shots themselves seem to create each other: This shot "makes" the next shot, which "makes" the next shot, etc. In this way, the Walter Murch who decided things initially gradually recedes until, finally, there comes a point where he has become invisible and the characters take over, the shots, the emotion, the story seem to take over. Sometimes—the best times—this process reaches the point where I can look at the scene and say, "I didn't have anything to do with that—it just created itself."

As far as the color balance of the final prints goes, I've had a few good experiences, but many have been frustrating for one reason or another. The worst thing is that the labs show the film at twenty-four frames per second (and sometimes even at thirty-two fps) without the ability to stop or go backward. You are sitting there and saying: "That shot should be redder." "Which one?" "The close-up of the foot." But already eight shots have gone by. Most often, the impression you get is that they are doing this as a courtesy just to keep you quiet.

One way that works for me, where you can really see what's going on and get specific with your notes about color, is to take the workprint and the first answer print and put them in sync over a light box of the correct color temperature. There is something about a low level of light coming through a piece of film that enables you to see tonalities that are almost invisible if you're looking at a bright screen of projected light. There may be a residual greenness, you know, but you look at the film in a viewing theater and you'll say, "I don't know. Is that shot a little green? Or is it too blue?" And, of course, before you have decided, you are looking at something else. If you work with the light-box system, the green will just leap out, especially if you've got your original workprint there for comparison. And you can stop, go forward, go backward, etc.

If you are fortunate enough to be working with a good color timer at a good laboratory, of course, it is like any sort of successful collaboration.

Test Screenings: Referred Pain

Toward the end of the editing process on *Julia*, Fred Zinnemann observed that he felt the director and the editor, alone with the film for months and months, could only go ninety percent of the way toward the finished film—that what was needed for the last ten percent was "the participation of the audience," whom he saw as his final collaborators. Not in the sense that he would respond to them blindly, but that he felt their presence was helpful as a corrective, to keep certain obsessions from becoming corrosive and to point out blind spots that may have developed through over-familiarity with the material.

This has certainly been my experience: All of the films I have worked on have been tested before large audiences except for *The Conversation* and *Unbearable Lightness.* We had screenings of them, of course, but we never had wide-open, public screenings. Francis Coppola in particular has always been an enthusiastic supporter of screening his films almost at any stage, almost no matter how unfinished they were.

Rough screenings would be for small groups of about ten people whom he knew, mixed with two or three people who were strangers. The strangers would have no previous idea of what this film was about, and he would question them afterward, on a one-to-one basis, to compare their opinions to the reaction of the people who did know about the film.

Fred Zinnemann, by contrast, would show *Julia* to a preview audience only when it was technically completely finished, with a cut negative and optical sound track. He was perfectly prepared to change it after that, but he doesn't believe that general audiences can completely discount visible splices, color mismatches, and incomplete sound tracks, and I agree with him.

Even with technically finished films, public previews are tricky things. You can learn a tremendous amount from them, but you have to be cautious about direct interpretations of what people have to say to you, particularly on those cards they fill out after the screening. I'm extremely suspicious of those. The most helpful thing of all is simply learning how *you* feel when the film is being shown to 600 people who have never seen it before. Emotionally, it seems like some big hand has come and grabbed you by the hair, picked you up, and put you down ninety degrees to one side. And you think, "Oh God, look at *that.*" It's as if up to this moment you have been constructing a building but always standing in front of it to evaluate it. Now all of a sudden you are looking at the side of the building and seeing things you seem to have never seen before.

You shouldn't blindly follow what you learn from these test screenings any more than you should anything else. What can you learn from the differences *between* the previous screenings and this one? Given these two headings, where is the North Pole? Test screenings are just a way to find out where you are.

There was one procedure on *Julia* that, unfortunately, I have never seen repeated. We had a person sitting at a table in the lobby of the preview theater with a sign in front of him that said, "If you want to talk to us on the telephone after a few days, leave your number here." And then those conversations were transcribed and added into the survey. If you are going to do previews and listen to what people have to say, that's the way to do it—after they have had a day or two to let the film sink in. Don't look at what people write in the heat of the moment—you get a reaction, but it is a skewed reaction. There's a lot of what is medically called "referred pain" in that process.

When you go to a doctor and tell him that you have a pain in your elbow, it is the quack who takes out his scalpel and starts to operate on the elbow. Then you wind up with not only the original pain but probably a pain in your wrist and your shoulder as well. Whereas an experienced doctor studies you, takes an x-ray, and determines that the cause of the pain is probably a pinched nerve up in your shoulder—you just happen to feel it in your elbow. The pain in the shoulder has been "referred" to the elbow. Audience reactions are like that. When you ask the direct question, "What was your least favorite scene?" and eighty percent of the people are in agreement about one scene they do not like, the impulse is to "fix" the scene or cut it out. But the chances are that that scene is fine. Instead, the problem may be that the audience simply didn't understand something that they needed to know for the scene to work.

So, instead of fixing the scene itself, you might clarify some exposition that happens five minutes earlier. Don't necessarily operate on the elbow: instead, discover if nerves are being pinched somewhere else. But the audience will never tell you that directly. They will simply tell you where the pain is, not the source of the pain.

Editing decisions become particularly acute in the last days before the film is released, since changes made now will be permanent. If you, as the editor, have a particularly strong feeling about something at this stage, you should try to make your point as forcefully and convincingly as you can—perhaps you stay late and do a test version of your idea, sketch something out—but you also need to have discretion, a sense of who you are dealing with, and present your ideas to the director or producer in the right context. And how you go about this has to do with your whole working history, how you were hired, how much you respect the director, how much the director respects you.

I remember one moment particularly, after the previews of *Julia*, when Fred Zinnemann and I were debating what final changes to make in the structure of the beginning, which seemed to have been difficult for the audience to follow. The opening reel of the film had a nested sequence of flashbacks—a memory of a memory of a memory of a memory—and it was perhaps one too many. I suggested eliminating of one scene that occupied a unique time-frame in the film's structure (one that was never reprised), and we decided to remove this, since it meant that the scenes that were left would consequently sort themselves into a more graspable sequence. As I was undoing the splices (and they made a little screech as they came apart, almost as if they were crying out in pain), Zinnemann looked thoughtfully at what was happening and observed in an almost offhand way, "You know, when I first read this scene in the script, I knew that I could do this film."

I hesitated briefly, looked at him, and then continued undoing the splices. But my heart was in my throat because at that stage in the process you do not know; you can only have *faith* that what you are doing is the right thing. Were we mistakenly cutting out the heart of the film, or were we snipping off the umbilical cord?

In retrospect, I believe it *was* the umbilical cord and that we were right to remove it: The scene did have an essential function at one point, which was to connect Fred Zinnemann to the project, but once that connection had been made and Zinnemann's sensibility had flowed through that scene into all the other scenes in the film, it could finally be removed without any harm.

But things like that do give you pause.

Don't Worry, It's Only a Movie

Earlier I asked the question, "Why do cuts work?" We *know* that they do. And yet it is still surprising when you think about it because of the violence of what is actually taking place: At the instant of the cut, there is a total and instantaneous discontinuity of the field of vision.

I recall once coming back to the editing room after a few weeks in the mixing theater (where all movements are smooth and incremental) and being appalled at the brutality of the process of cutting. The "patient" is pinned to the slab and: Whack! Either/Or! This not That! In or Out! We chop up the poor film in a miniature guillotine and then stick the dismembered pieces together like Dr. Frankenstein's monster. The difference (the miraculous difference) is that out of this apparent butchery our creation can sometimes gain not only a life but a soul as well. It is all the more amazing because the instantaneous displacement achieved by the cut is not anything that we experience in ordinary life.

We are accustomed to such things, of course, in music (Beethoven was the innovator and master of this) as well as in our own thoughts—the way one realization will suddenly overwhelm everything else, to be, in turn, replaced by yet another. But in the dramatic arts—theater, ballet, opera—there didn't seem to be any way to achieve total instantaneous displacement: stage machinery can only move so fast, after all. *So why do cuts work?* Do they have some hidden foundation in our own experience, or are they an invention that suits the convenience of filmmakers and people have just, somehow, become used to them?

Well, although "day-to-day" reality appears to be continuous, there *is* that other world in which we spend perhaps a third of our lives: the "night-to-night" reality of dreams. And the images in dreams are much more fragmented, intersecting in much stranger and more abrupt ways than the images of waking reality—ways that approximate, at least, the interaction produced by cutting.

Perhaps the explanation is as simple as that: We accept the cut because it resembles the way images are juxtaposed in our dreams. In fact, the abruptness of the cut may be one of the key determinants in actually *producing* the similarity between films and dreams. In the darkness of the theater, we say to ourselves, in effect, "This looks like reality, but it cannot be reality because it is so visually discontinuous; therefore, it must be a dream."

(Along those lines, it is revealing that the words a parent uses to comfort a child frightened by a nightmare—"Don't worry, darling, it's only a dream"—are almost the same words used to comfort a child frightened by a film—"Don't worry, darling, it's only a movie." Frightening dreams and films have a similar power to overwhelm the defenses that are otherwise effective against equally frightening books, paintings, music. For instance, it is hard to imagine this phrase: "Don't worry, darling, it's only a painting.")

The problem with all this is that the comparison of films and dreams is interesting, probably true, but relatively barren of practical fruits: We still know so little about the nature of dreams that the observation comes to a stop once it has been made.

Something to consider, though, is the possibility that there may be a part of our waking reality where we actually do experience something like cuts, and where daylight images are somehow brought in closer, more discontinuous, juxtaposition than might otherwise seem to be the case.

I began to get a glimmer of this on my first picture-editing job—*The Conversation* (1974)—when I kept finding that Gene Hackman (Harry Caul in the film) would blink very close to the point where I had decided to cut. It was interesting, but I didn't know what to make of it.

Then, one morning after I had been working all night, I went out to get some breakfast and happened to walk past the window of a Christian Science Reading Room, where the front page of the *Monitor* featured an interview with John Huston. I stopped to read it, and one thing struck me forcefully because it related exactly to this question of the blink:

"To me, the perfect film is as though it were unwinding behind your eyes, and your eyes were projecting it themselves, so that you were seeing what you wished to see. Film is like thought. It's the closest to thought process of any art.

"Look at that lamp across the room. Now look back at me. Look back at that lamp. Now look back at me again. Do you see what you did? You *blinked.* Those are *cuts.* After the first look, you know that there's no reason to pan continuously from me to the lamp because you know what's in between. Your mind cut the scene. First you behold the lamp. *Cut.* Then you behold me."[12]

What Huston asks us to consider is a physiological mechanism—the blink—that interrupts the apparent visual continuity of our perceptions: My head may move smoothly from one side of the room to the other, but, in fact, I am cutting the flow of visual images into significant bits, the better to juxtapose and compare those bits—"lamp" and "face" in Huston's example—without irrelevant information getting in the way.

Of course there are limits to the kind of juxtapositions I can make this way—I can't jump forward or backward in time and space (that is the prerogative of dreams and films).[13] But even so, the visual displacements available to me just by turning my head (from the Grand Canyon in front of me to the forest behind me, or even from one side of this room to the other) are sometimes quite great.

---

[12] *Christian Science Monitor,* August 11, 1973. John Huston interviewed by Louise Sweeney.

[13] But see footnote #16.

After I read that article, I started observing people, watching when they blinked, and I began to discover something much different than what they tell you in high-school biology, which is that the blink is simply a means to moisten the surface of the eye. If that's all it is, then for each environment and each individual there would be a purely mechanical, predictable interval between blinks depending on the humidity, temperature, wind speed, etc. You would only blink when your eye began to get too dry, and that would be a constant number of seconds for each environment. This is clearly not the case: People will sometimes keep their eyes open for minutes at a time—at other times they will blink repeatedly—with many variations in between. The question then is, "What is causing them to blink?"

On the one hand, I'm sure you've all been confronted by someone who was so angry that he didn't blink at all: This is a person, I believe, in the grip of a single thought that he holds (and that holds him), inhibiting the urge and need to blink.[14] And then there is the opposite kind of anger that causes someone to blink every second or so: This time, the person is being assailed simultaneously by many conflicting emotions and thoughts, and is desperately (but unconsciously) using those blinks to try to separate these thoughts, sort things out, and regain some kind of control.

[14] There is that telling phrase from classic cowboy (and now diplomatic) stand-offs: "he blinked." The loser in this mental game of chicken could not hold fast to his single position and instead allowed some other thought to intrude at the critical moment. The blink signals the moment he relinquished his primary thought.

So it seems to me that our rate of blinking is somehow geared more to our emotional state and to the nature and frequency of our thoughts than to the atmospheric environment we happen to find ourselves in. Even if there is no head movement (as there was in Huston's example), the blink is either *something that helps an internal separation of thought to take place,* or it is *an involuntary reflex accompanying the mental separation that is taking place anyway.*[15]

And not only is the *rate* of blinking significant, but so is the actual *instant* of the blink itself. Start a conversation with somebody and watch when they blink. I believe you will find that your listener will blink at the precise moment he or she "gets" the idea of what you are saying, not an instant earlier or later. Why would this be? Well, speech is full of unobserved grace notes and elaborations—the conversational equivalents of "Dear Sir" and "Yours Sincerely"—and the essence of what we have to say is often sandwiched between an introduction and a conclusion. The blink will take place either when the listener realizes our "introduction" is finished and that now we are going to say something significant, or it will happen when he feels we are "winding down" and not going to say anything more significant for the moment.

And that blink will occur where a cut could have happened, had the conversation been filmed. Not a frame earlier or later.

So we entertain an idea, or a linked sequence of ideas, and we blink to separate and punctuate that idea from what follows. Similarly—in film—a shot

---

[15] Dr. John Stern of Washington University in St. Louis has recently (1987) published experimental work in the psycho-physiology of the blink that seems to confirm this.

presents us with an idea, or a sequence of ideas, and the cut is a "blink" that separates and punctuates those ideas.[16] At the moment you decide to cut, what you are saying is, in effect, "I am going to bring this idea to an end and start something new." It is important to emphasize that the cut by *itself* does not create the "blink moment"—the tail does not wag the dog. If the cut is well-placed, however, the more extreme the visual discontinuity—from dark interior to bright exterior, for instance—the more thorough the effect of punctuation will be.

At any rate, I believe "filmic" juxtapositions are taking place in the real world not only when we dream but also when we are awake. And, in fact, I would go so far as to say that these juxtapositions are not accidental mental artifacts but part of the method we use to make sense of the world: We must render visual reality discontinuous, otherwise perceived reality would resemble an almost incomprehensible string of letters without word separation or punctuation. When we sit in the dark theater, then we find edited film a (surprisingly) familiar experience. "More like thought than anything else," in Huston's words.[17]

---

[16] This can occur regardless of how big or small the "idea" happens to be. For instance, the idea could be as simple as "she moves quickly to the left."

[17] William Stokoe makes an intriguing comparison between the techniques of film editing and American Sign Language: "In signed language, narrative is no longer linear. Instead, the essence is to cut from a normal view to a close-up to a distant shot to a close-up again, even including flashback and flash-forward scenes, exactly as a movie editor works. Not only is signing arranged more like edited film than like written narration, but also each signer is placed very much as a camera: the field of vision and angle of view are directed but variable." William Stokoe, *Language in Four Dimensions*, New York Academy of Sciences (1979).

Dragnet

If it is true that our rates and rhythms of blinking refer directly to the rhythm and sequence of our inner emotions and thoughts, then those rates and rhythms are insights into our inner selves and, therefore, as characteristic of each of us as our signatures. So if an actor is successful at projecting himself into the emotions and thoughts of a character, his blinks will *naturally and spontaneously* occur at the point that the character's blinks would have occurred in real life.[18]

I believe this is what I was finding with Hackman's performance in *The Conversation*—he had assumed the character of Harry Caul, was thinking a series of Harry's thoughts the way Harry would think them, and, therefore, was blinking in rhythm with those thoughts. And since I was absorbing the rhythms he

---

[18] One of the things about unsuccessful acting is that the actor's blinks seem to come at the "wrong" times. Although you may not notice this consciously, the rhythm of the actor's blinks don't match the rhythm of thoughts you would expect from the character he is playing. In fact, a bad actor is probably not thinking anything like what the character would be thinking. Instead: "I wonder what the director thinks of me, I wonder if I look okay," or "What's my next line?"

was giving me and trying to think similar thoughts myself, my cut points were naturally aligning themselves with his "blink points." In a sense, I had rerouted my neural circuitry so that the semi-involuntary command to blink caused me instead to hit the stop button on the editing machine.

To that same end, one of the disciplines I follow is to choose the "out point" of a shot by marking it in real time. If I can't do this—if I can't hit that same frame repeatedly at twenty-four frames per second—I know there is something wrong in my approach to the shot, and I adjust my thinking until I find a frame I *can* hit. I never permit myself to select the "out point" by inching back and forth, comparing one frame with another to get the best match. That method—for me, at any rate—is guaranteed to produce a rhythmic "tone deafness" in the film.

Anyway, another one of your tasks as an editor is this "sensitizing" of yourself to the rhythms that the (good) actor gives you, and then finding ways to extend these rhythms into territory not covered by the actor himself, so that the pacing of the film as a whole is an elaboration of those patterns of thinking and feeling. And one of the many ways you assume those rhythms is by noticing—consciously or unconsciously—where the actor blinks.

There is a way of editing that ignores all of these questions, what I would call the "Dragnet" system, from the 1950s TV series of the same name.

The policy of the show seemed to be to keep every word of dialogue on screen. When someone had finished speaking, there was a brief pause and then a cut to the person, who was now about to talk, and when he in turn finished speaking there was a cut back to the first person who nodded his head or said something, and then when *that* person was finished, they cut back again, etc. It extended to single words. "Have you been downtown yet?" *Cut.* "No." *Cut.* "When are you going downtown?" *Cut.* "Tomorrow." *Cut.* "Have you seen your son?" *Cut.* "No, he didn't come home last night." *Cut.* "What time does he usually come home?" *Cut.* "Two o'clock." At the time, when it first came out, this technique created a sensation for its apparently hard-boiled, police-blotter realism.

The "Dragnet" system is a simple way to edit, but it is a shallow simplicity that doesn't reflect the grammar of complex exchanges that go on all the time in even the most ordinary conversations. If you're observing a dialogue between two people, you will not focus your attention solely on the person who is speaking. Instead, while *that person is still talking,* you will turn to look at the listener to find out what he thinks of what is being said. The question is, "When exactly do you turn?"

There are places in a conversation where it seems we almost physically *cannot* blink or turn our heads (since we are still receiving important information), and there are other places where we *must* blink or turn away in order to make better sense of what we have received. And I would suggest that there are similar points in every scene where the cut *cannot* or *must* occur, and for the same reasons. Every shot has potential "cut points" the way a tree has branches, and once you have identified them, you will choose different points depending on what the audience has been thinking up to that moment and what you want them to think next.

For instance, by cutting away from a certain character *before* he finishes speaking, I might encourage the audience to think only about the face value of what he said. On the other hand, if I linger on the character *after* he finishes speaking, I allow the audience to see, from the expression in his eyes, that he is probably not telling the truth, and they will think differently about him and what he said. But since it takes a *certain amount of time* to make that observation, I cannot cut away from the character too early: Either I cut away while he is speaking (branch number one) or I hold until the audience realizes he is lying (branch number two), but *I cannot cut in between those two branches*—to do so would either seem too long or not long enough. The branch points are fixed organically by the rhythm of the shot itself and by what the audience has been thinking up to that moment in the film,[19] but I am free to select one or the other of them (or yet another one further on) depending on what realization I want the audience to make.

In this way, you should be able to cut from the speaker to the listener and vice versa in psychologically interesting, complex, and "correct" patterns that reflect the kinds of shifts of attention and realization that go on in real life: In this way, you establish a

[19] One way to shift the actual branch points themselves is to place the shot in a different context, where the audience will be thinking (and noticing) different things.

rhythm that counterpoints and underscores the ideas being expressed or considered. And one of the tools to identify exactly where these cut points, these "branches," may be is to compare them to our patterns of blinking, which have been underscoring the rhythm of our thoughts for tens of thousands, perhaps millions, of years of human history. Where you feel comfortable blinking—if you are really listening to what is being said—is where the cut will feel right.

So there are really three problems wrapped up together:

1) identifying a series of potential cut points (and comparisons with the blink can help you do this),

2) determining what effect each cut point will have on the audience, and

3) choosing which of those effects is the correct one for the film.

I believe the sequence of thoughts—that is to say, the rhythm and rate of cutting—should be appropriate to whatever the audience is watching at the moment. The average "real-world" rate of blinking is somewhere between the extremes of four and forty blinks per minute. If you are in an actual fight, you will be blinking dozens of times a minute because you are thinking dozens of conflicting thoughts a minute—and so when you are watching a fight in a film, there should be dozens of cuts per minute.[20] In

---

[20] This would make the audience participate emotionally in the fight itself. If, on the other hand, you wanted to create an objective distance—to have the audience observe the fight as a phenomenon in itself—then you would reduce the number of cuts considerably.

fact, statistically the two rates—of real-life blinking and of film cutting—are close enough for comparison: Depending on how it is staged, a convincing action sequence might have around twenty-five cuts a minute, whereas a dialogue scene would still feel "normal" (in an American film) averaging six cuts per minute or less.

You should be right with the blinks, perhaps leading them ever so slightly. I certainly don't expect the audience to blink at every cut—the cut point should be a *potential* blink point. In a sense, by cutting, by this sudden displacement of the visual field, you are blinking *for* the audience: You achieve the immediate juxtaposition of two concepts for them—what they achieve in the real world by blinking, as in Huston's example.

Your job is partly to anticipate, partly to control the thought processes of the audience. To give them what they want and/or what they need just before they have to "ask" for it—to be surprising yet self-evident at the same time. If you are too far behind or ahead of them, you create problems, but if you are right with them, leading them ever so slightly, the flow of events feels natural and exciting at the same time.

A Galaxy of Winking Dots

Along these lines, it would be fascinating to take an infrared film of an audience and find out when and in what patterns people blink when they are watching a movie. My hunch is that if an audience is really in the grip of a film, they are going to be thinking (and therefore blinking) with the rhythm of the film.

There is a wonderful effect that you can produce if you shine infrared light directly out in line with the lens of a camera. All animal eyes (including human eyes) will bounce a portion of that light directly back into the camera, and you will see bright glowing dots where the eyes are: It is a version of the "red-eye" effect in family snapshots taken with flashbulbs.

If you took a high-contrast infrared motion picture of an audience watching a film, placing the camera on stage and aligning the light source directly with the camera, you would see a galaxy of these dots against a field of black. And when someone in the audience blinked, you would see a momentary interruption in a pair of these dots.

If it were true, if there *were* times when those thousand dots winked more or less in unison, the film-maker would have an extremely powerful tool at his disposal. Coherent blinking would be a strong indication that the audience was thinking together, and that the film was working. But when the blinking became scattered, it would indicate that he may have lost his audience, that they had begun to think about where to go for dinner, or whether their car was parked in a safe place, etc.

When people are deeply "in" a film, you'll notice that nobody coughs at certain moments, even though they may have a cold. If the coughing were purely an autonomic response to smoke or congestion, it would be randomly constant, no matter what was happening on screen. But the audience holds back at certain moments, and I'm suggesting that blinking is something like coughing in this sense. There is a famous live recording of pianist Sviatoslav Richter playing Mussorgsky's *Pictures at an Exhibition* during a flu epidemic in Bulgaria many years ago. It is just as plain as day what's going on: While he was playing certain passages, no one coughed. At those moments, he was able to suppress, with his artistry, the coughing impulse of 1,500 sick people.

I think this subconscious attention to the blink is also something that you would probably find as a hidden factor in everyday life. One thing that may make you nervous about a particular person is that you feel, without knowing it, that his blinking is wrong. "He's blinking too much" or "He's not blinking enough" or "He's blinking at the wrong time." Which means he is not really listening to you, thinking along with you.

Whereas somebody who is really focused on what you are saying will blink at the "right" places at the "right" rate, and you will feel comfortable in this person's presence. I think we know these things intuitively, subconsciously, without having to be told, and I wouldn't be surprised to find that it is part of our built-in strategy for dealing with each other.

When we suggest that someone is a bad actor, we are certainly not saying that he is a bad human being; we are just saying that this person is not as fully *in* the character as he wants us to believe, and he's nervous about it. You can see this clearly in political campaigns, where there is sometimes a vivid distinction between who somebody is and who they want the voters to believe they are: Something will always be "wrong" with the rate and moment that these people blink.

That brings me back to one of the central responsibilities of the editor, which is to establish an interesting, coherent rhythm of emotion and thought—on the tiniest and the largest scales—that allows the audience to trust, to give themselves to the film. Without their knowing why, a poorly edited film will cause the audience to hold back, unconsciously saying to themselves, "There's something scattered and nervous about the way the film is thinking, the way it presents itself. I don't want to think that way; therefore, I'm not going to give as much of myself to the film as I might." Whereas a good film that is well-edited seems like an exciting extension and elaboration of the audience's own feelings and thoughts, and they will therefore give themselves to it, as it gives itself to them.

AFTER WORD

DIGITAL FILM EDITING

Past, Present, and Imagined Future

In the first quarter of the twentieth century, the film editor's room was a quiet place, equipped only with a rewind bench, a pair of scissors, a magnifying glass, and the knowledge that the distance from the tip of one's nose to the fingers of the outstretched hand represented about three seconds. In those manual, pre-mechanical days—roughly 1900-1925—the cutting room was a relatively tranquil tailor's shop in which time was the cloth.

The editor had seen the film projected when it first came from the laboratory, and now she (many editors in those days were women) re-examined the still frames with a magnifying glass, recalling how they looked in motion, and cut with scissors where she thought correct. Patiently and somewhat intuitively, she stitched the fabric of her film together, joining with paper clips the shots that were to be later cemented together by a technician down the hall.

She then projected the assembly with the director and producer, took notes, and returned to her room to make further adjustments, shortening this and lengthening that, like a second fitting of a suit. This new version was projected in turn, and the cycle was repeated over and over until the fit was as perfect as she could make it.

It's startling to recall that the humble Moviola (that frog-green machine found in virtually every editing room over the last seventy years) was rejected by many editors of the pre-mechanical age as too expensive, noisy, and cumbersome—even dangerous, since film in those days was made of cellulose nitrate, an extremely flammable substance chemically similar to dynamite. Still worse (if that's possible), the Moviola's main attribute—the ability to study the *motion* of the images, frame by frame—was dismissed as an irrelevant crutch that would simply get in the way of the work to be done.

After an initial attempt to penetrate the industry in the early 1920s, the machine was offered to the general public as a way of viewing home movies—hence the friendly name *Moviola*, reminiscent of the then-popular *Victrola* record player. It probably would have withered away as a footnote to film history had not a fortuitous technical breakthrough occurred in 1927: sound.

Sound—The Talking Picture—was the Trojan horse that ushered in the rackety Mechanical Age of editing. No magnifying glass or three-second rule could help the editor lip-read those silent frames, and the "double-headed" (picture and sound) Moviola was wheeled through the studio gates, where it and its more sophisticated European children—German Steenbeck and KEM, Italian Prevost, and French Moritone—have been ever since.

Until now.

Now, at the beginning of the twenty-first century, film editing is in the midst of transforming itself from a mechanical process to an electronic one, and the Moviola is increasingly found—if it is found at all—as an amusing and nostalgic artifact displayed in the foyers of the studio post-production departments.

In 1992, when this book was first published, almost all films were still being edited mechanically, although the electronic wave was building an unstoppable momentum. Now, at the beginning of the twenty-first century, the situation is reversed: Almost all films are being edited electronically, on computers.

This doesn't mean that film *itself*—the sprocketed 35mm strip of celluloid—has disappeared. It is still (for a few more years) the medium that captures the image in the first place, and it is still (perhaps for a few years less) the medium that delivers the image to the theaters.

The electronic systems most commonly employed today are: the *Avid,* the most thoroughly developed and by far the most commonly used system; *Final Cut Pro,* a program recently developed by Apple that runs on Macintosh operating systems; and *Lightworks,* which runs only on Windows. There are some functional differences among the three, but they work essentially the same way:

1) **Once the film is shot** and developed in the lab, it is copied into the computer through a process of *digitization.* This allows every frame of the film to be stored on a hard disk,

in very much the same way that graphics programs, such as Photoshop, store digitized photographs.

2) **Each frame of the film** is given a specific number, or *address,* in a database. This allows the editor to play these frames in any sequence. The software keeps a record of these decisions, which can be played repeatedly, and changed at will, very much the way text can be "played back" and modified in a word processor.

3) **Once the right sequence** is decided, the program will print out a list of those decisions, called an *edit decision list.* This list allows the 35mm film to be conformed, using traditional editing tools, to match what is in the computer. The finished film can then be shown in a theater, on conventional projectors.

But why would anyone choose to go through these contortions? Why not just edit the film itself, especially since you begin with film and end with film? Why give up a perfectly good way of making films, one that had been perfected over many years and used (brilliantly) to make all of the classic films that we know and love?

Those are good questions. Or at least they were good questions eight or ten years ago, and ones that many editors asked themselves at the time.

In fact, some still do: Three of the most celebrated filmmakers of the last third of the twentieth century—

Steven Spielberg, David Lynch, and Alan Parker—still prefer to edit on film. Spielberg has gone so far as to buy a dozen Moviolas with spare parts and secure the services of dedicated technicians to keep them in perfect working order for the foreseeable future

In the following pages, I would like to review how this electronic-digital revolution has come about; why it came about despite its complexity and the resistance of influential people; and to examine some of the long-term technical and artistic implications of a completely digitized film industry.

Astronomical Numbers

But first I'd like to take a moment to emphasize the astronomical number of ways that images can be combined in a motion picture. This has always been the case, no matter what editing system is used: manual, mechanical, or electronic.

If a scene is photographed with only two shots—one each from two different camera positions (A and B, let's say)—you can choose one or the other or a combination of both. As a result, you have at least four ways of using these two images: A, B, A+B, and B+A. However, once the number gets much larger than two shots—and a director might shoot twenty-five shots for an average scene—the number of possible combinations quickly becomes astronomical.

It turns out there is a formula for this. Here it is:

$$C = (e \times n!) - 1$$

"C" is the minimum number of different ways a scene can be assembled using "n," all of the shots the director has taken for that scene; "e" is the transcendental number 2.71828..., one of those mysterious constants (like π) you might remember from high school. And the exclamation point after the "n" (the one instance where mathematics gets emotional!) stands for *factorial*, which means you multiply together all the numbers up to and including the number in question.

For instance, the factorial of 4 = 1x2x3x4 = 24. The factorial of 6 = 1x2x3x4x5x6 = 720, so you see the results get big pretty fast. The factorial of 25 is a very large number, something like 15 billion billion million—15 followed by 24 zeros. Multiply that by "e" and you get (roughly) 40 followed by 24 zeros. Minus one.

So a scene made up of only twenty-five shots can be edited in approximately 39,999,999,999,999,999,999, 999,999 different ways. In miles, this is twenty-five times the circumference of the observable universe.

If you had fifty-nine shots for a scene, which is not at all unusual, you would potentially have as many possible versions of that scene as there are subatomic particles in the entire universe! Some action sequences I've edited have had upwards of 250 shots, so you can imagine the kind of numbers involved: 88 followed by a solid page of zeros—91 of them.

Now, the vast majority of these versions would be complete junk. Like the old story of a million chimpanzees at a million typewriters, most of what they banged out would make no sense at all. On the other hand, even such a "small" number as 40 followed by 24 zeros is so huge that a tiny percentage of it (the potentially good versions) will still be overwhelmingly large. If only one version in every quadrillion makes sense, that still leaves 40 million possible versions. For just one scene. And a theatrical film usually has hundreds of scenes, which themselves can be (and frequently are) rearranged from their original script order.

So the queasy feeling in the pit of the stomach of every editor beginning a project is the recognition—conscious or not—of the immense number of choices he or she is facing. The numbers are so huge that there is no possibility of turning film editing into a kind of automated chess game, where all of the different options are evaluated before making a move. But electronic editing, more than the traditional mechanical methods, offers more and faster ways to cope with these super-astronomical numbers.

The Electronic Advantages

This is because what you are actually creating in the computer is a *virtual assembly*—the images themselves have not been disturbed, only the computer instructions for what to do with the images (remember the *edit decision list* mentioned earlier). This is a fundamental difference with the mechanical systems, which create what is rather dramatically termed a *destructive assembly* of the film. This simply means that, in mechanical editing, the *images* and the *information about the arrangement* of the images are one and the same thing: You automatically establish the information about the sequence of shots by putting those shots in a certain sequence. If this seems self-evident, well—it is! In computer editing, however, this is not the case: Information about the order of shots is held in a separate place from the shots themselves.

What this means is that every time you look at a sequence on a computer editing system, the images are being magically assembled for you *as you watch*. If you want to do something completely different with a scene, the system doesn't care at all—you are only changing the instructions, the recipe for this particular dish, not the dish itself. In a mechanical system, you have to undo version A before you can create version B (destroying version A in the process).

This crucial difference between digital and mechanical systems leads directly to the main selling points that have propelled electronic random-access editing systems forward and made them now generally accepted over the old mechanical systems.

Before we go any farther, let me quickly summarize these points:

- **Increased speed** is certainly the most important (and certainly the most frequently mentioned) attribute of electronic systems. Pure speed has appeal both to the studios, who want their films done quickly, and to editors, who are trying to pack as much creativity as they can into every hour that the producers will give them. "How fast is he?" is frequently the first question that will be asked about an editor, and any tool that can give an edge on speed will be welcomed. The quickness of electronic systems comes about for many reasons, mostly through the instant random-access to the material. In the old mechanical systems, a human being (the editor or the assistant) would have to locate and retrieve every shot. In a computer, it is only a mouse-click away.

- **Reduced cost** because it may eliminate the need for film workprint. For certain low-budget films, this might be an attractive option, since you can transfer directly from film negative to hard disk at roughly half the cost of making a positive workprint. Once the film is edited, you then need only print the takes that were included in the cut, which might reduce your workprint budget by ninety percent.
- **Fewer people** employed in the cutting room, since the computer automatically takes care of such things as filing trims, making lists, etc., that are usually handled by several assistants and apprentices. As we will see further on, this may not yet—practically speaking—be the case. But theoretically it is enticing.
- **Easier access** to the material. The traditional editing room has a certain medieval "crafts guild" feel to it, with a defined hierarchy and long training periods in obscure crafts—such as coding and reconstitution—that are reduced or eliminated in the digital domain. Simply stated, the goal of electronic editing is to make it as easy and accessible as word processing.

- **The director can review** all the material, in its original "uncut" state, even though it may simultaneously be included in the assemblies of many different versions of the film. Remember that the computer only creates a "virtual" assembly, not a "destructive" one. In the mechanical systems, once part of a shot is included in an assembly, the director is no longer able to see that shot in its uncut form.
- **A more civilized working environment** free from the rackety noise and "physicality" of the Moviola and film itself. The electronic image you are looking at does not get scratched, torn, burned, and is not physically spliced the way film is. You can see what you are doing more calmly and clearly, for as long as you care to keep doing it.
- **Preservation of different versions** of the film. Just as there are no trims to worry about, electronic editing is able to recall every attempted version of a scene and then file these for future reference. By comparison, in mechanical editing, there is no easy way to "go back" unless you make the deliberate, expensive, and time-consuming decision to copy the scene in question onto duplicating film or videotape.
- **Sophisticated use of sound:** Avid, Final Cut Pro, and Lightworks can all carry many tracks of sound along with the image and automatically maintain them in the correct relationship to the picture, no matter how many changes are made. Mechanical systems were limited, practically

speaking, to two or three tracks, and these had to be separately and somewhat laboriously conformed to changes in the picture. Also, and significantly, Avid can vary the loudness of any section of sound—fade it in or out and change its equalization—simulating the final mix. Mechanical systems can do none of this.

- **Integration with electronic special effects:** Electronic systems make it convenient to flow back and forth from the editing process to increasingly sophisticated electronic special effects. Traditional fades, dissolves, and wipes can be seen and evaluated instantly, of course, as well as any repositioning and cropping of the frame, reversals of action, speed-ups and slow-downs of action. But this is just the tip of the digital iceberg.

In breezily summarizing the bright side of the present situation at the beginning of a new century, I am necessarily minimizing the struggle that it took to get here. Electronic editing did not spring upon the world readymade and as artfully arranged as it now appears to be. Three decades of development were necessary to get things to their present state, and this in turn built on the previous seventy years of experience with mechanical editing. In addition, every one of the advantages listed above has its "evil twin"—a flip side that has the potential to cancel out the good. The problems encountered on the way, and the solutions (some successful, some not), help illuminate the inherent qualities of electronic filmmaking—and its potential future.

Digital: Back to the Future

My first exposure to computer-controlled editing came in 1968 and coincided—appropriately enough—with my introduction to Francis Coppola, who has been an innovator and champion of electronic cinema for more than thirty years. Francis, who had recently graduated from UCLA film school, and George Lucas, a fellow student with me at USC, were investigating an early CMX system down the street from where I was working in Hollywood (on a Moviola!).

It seemed clear to each of us, in our mid-twenties then, that this room—humming with expensive, relatively cumbersome equipment—was a glimpse of the future of film editing. And a few years later, after American Zoetrope had been launched in San Francisco, the three of us put together a proposal for using the CMX system to edit sections of *The Godfather*. Nothing came directly from that early effort—computer storage and access were, at the time, far too primitive and costly for the amount of footage generated by a feature film.

Development of many different competing systems—CMX, Montage, EditDroid, E-Pix, EMC, D-Vision, Avid, Lightworks, and a number of others—continued throughout the seventies and eighties. A tremendous amount of research and development was invested in these systems, particularly when you consider that, although professional *film* is an expensive medium, there is not a lot of professional *film equipment* in the world (compared, for instance, to medical equipment). And since the standards and tolerances of film equipment are extremely high, there has not been a significant amount of money to be made in improving what already exists.

Television equipment, on the other hand, offers a tremendous world-wide potential for profit and innovation at both the professional and consumer levels. The present wave of interest in electronic postproduction comes partly from those who envision a technical merging of the two worlds (film and television, professional and consumer), and hence a considerable increase in the amount of money to be made. Avid, for instance, has for some time been delivering completely digital TV news stations throughout Europe for around $1 million each, and its yearly turnover in this area is approximately $200 million.

But electronic editing has not been promoted only by the hardware developers. A strong push has also come from the filmmakers themselves: George Lucas, Oliver Stone, Jim Cameron, Steven Soderbergh, Carroll Ballard, Bernardo Bertolucci, Francis Coppola, and many others experimented with different electronic systems to edit their films. Lucas went so far as to become a developer himself throughout the 1980s, with his innovative EditDroid system. And short of actually creating marketable hardware, Francis Coppola has been one of the leading advocates and users of electronic editing from the mid-1970s to the present. The desire among the filmmakers has been less about saving money and more to do with increasing editing speed and, most significantly, multiplying creative options.

The resistance to electronic editing came mostly from experienced professional editors and directors who observed that the merging of film and television was not a *fait accompli* (and who might resist it for temperamental reasons even if it were). They were comfortable with all the well-worn peculiarities of their mechanical systems, on which they had waged and won many battles, and were reluctant to embrace a completely different system whose benefits had not been proven.

My own experience with electronic editing throughout these formative years was as interested partisan and occasional practitioner. Six years after our proposal for using the CMX system on *The Godfather,* Francis installed a simple linear video-editing system (no computer, no random-access) on which we could experiment with different story structures for *Apocalypse Now,* and I used it to help visualize the series of overlapping four-element dissolves in the first reel of that film. Other than that, *Apocalypse* (all 1.2 million feet of workprint, almost seven tons of film and sound!) was mechanically edited on two Moviolas (by Richie Marks and Jerry Greenberg) and two KEM "8-plates" (by Lisa Fruchtman and myself).

After *Apocalypse,* Francis and I didn't have the opportunity to work together again on a feature until *The Godfather, Part III* (1990). Although I had started using a computerized database for editorial record management in 1982, I continued to edit directly on film (on Moviolas, KEM, and Steenbecks) throughout the 1980s.

Francis, though, used linear video editing on all his films during this period, from *One From the Heart* (1981) to *Tucker* (1988). His "Silverfish"—a customized Airstream motorhome packed with electronic editing and monitoring equipment—first made its appearance on *One From the Heart*.

By the time of *The Godfather, Part III,* however, Francis had moved from the relatively primitive linear videotape systems up to a true random-access, computer-controlled (though still tape-based) Montage editing system. Lisa Fruchtman started using it in the fall of 1989 to put together the first assembly of the film, and another system was added when Barry Malkin joined the film in the spring of 1990. But when I joined the crew a few months later, in August, it just didn't seem practical to add a third system, so I worked directly on film, using a KEM "8-plate." A few months later I did use the Montage, with the help of Gus Carpenter, to assemble the *Godfather Trilogy,* a ten-hour compilation of all three *Godfather* films.

In Marin County, across the Golden Gate Bridge from Francis's Zoetrope Studios, George Lucas had mobilized the considerable resources of LucasFilm, starting around 1981, to pursue research and development of his ambitious laserdisc-based EditDroid electronic editing system, and was able to put it to practical use by the mid-1980s. Carroll Ballard and his editor, Michael Chandler, used it on Ballard's *Wind* (1991), and the system was used, whole or in part, on such features as Steven Soderbergh's *Kafka* (1991) and *King of the Hill* (1993), Oliver Stone's *The Doors* (1991), John McTiernan's *Medicine Man* (1992), and James Brooks' *I'll Do Anything* (1993). In addition, LucasFilm's entire *Young Indiana Jones* television series (1991-1995) was assembled on EditDroid. But as luck would have it, no LucasFilm feature ever used the LucasFilm system, because by the mid-1990s, both EditDroid and the functionally similar Montage system had been overwhelmed by technical developments that were leading to the eventual pre-eminence of completely digital systems such as Avid and Lightworks.

Transition from Analog to Digital

It was not technically feasible to digitize the huge amount of film generated by the average feature onto the relatively primitive hard drives of the 1980s. So the expedient solution was to store the film on conventional analog media, such as videotape or laserdisc, and use the computers only to manipulate the information about *what to do* with those images: in effect, to have the computer control the banks of analog machines on which the images were kept. EditDroid used laserdiscs as a storage medium and Montage used videotape cassettes, but the operational principle was essentially the same for both systems, which might be called "analog-electronic."

In the late-1980s, because of advances in computer memory technology, it became possible to digitize film images directly onto the computer's hard disk. This is the central innovation underlying both Avid and Lightworks, which might be described as "digital-electronic."

Because they have everything—*media* and *information about that media*—"under one roof," so to speak, these digital systems were inherently more efficient, productive, and flexible than their analog predecessors. And the editors *themselves* could digitize the film quickly and efficiently from videotapes of the dailies, rather than sending the film out to professional services to be copied onto laserdiscs or multiple VHS tapes.

The digital machines were rightly criticized in the early stages of their development for having poor image quality compared to, say, the EditDroid laserdiscs, but as hard-disk memory became precipitously less expensive during the 1990s, the quality of the digitized image correspondingly increased, to the extent that both EditDroid and Montage found the digital competition increasingly difficult to overcome.

Despite all these editing system developments, however, we found ourselves, in the mid-1990s, stuck in a lingering electro-mechanical "transition phase"—one that lasted years longer than I would have guessed when I was so dazzled by the CMX back in 1968. After all, 2001 was only a few years away, the 33 1/3 LP was history, word processors had universally replaced electric typewriters, and here we were still listening to the clattering of the Moviola's Maltese Cross, with scratched film all over the floor and splicers, tape, trim bins, and grease pencils filling the editing room. I believe the awareness of this odd technological lag was one of the strongest psychological undercurrents pushing electronic editing forward. The persistence of the Moviola into the last decade of the twentieth century is about as surprising as seeing an old manual Underwood typewriter being loaded onto the Space Shuttle.

What was going on?

Development Problems

Simply stated, most of the early non-linear systems were oversold, particularly regarding the huge demands that feature films made on computer storage and processing power. And the difficulties of getting the film into these systems, and then accurately out again, was considerably underestimated.

- **The amount of memory** that early non-linear machines had was limited. You simply couldn't store the entire film in one gulp, so it all had to be broken down into chunks, which caused serious procedural and creative dislocations. Moving from one section of the film to another involved swapping the media (hard disk, laserdisc, or tape) on which the film was stored. *Godfather III,* which was edited on a Montage tape-based non-linear system, had this problem as late as 1990.
- **A bottleneck** existed in the workflow. The early machines were so expensive that you could usually afford just one per film. As a result, the editor and the assistant had to work split shifts—which meant the assistant worked at night, with all the problems that you'd expect from that kind of arrangement. Even if a film could afford more than one machine, there was no way that those machines could share access to the same media.
- **It was complicated, inconvenient, and expensive** to get the image "on line" in the analog-electronic systems (EditDroid, Montage). Laserdiscs of the dailies had to be specially made

for EditDroid, and dozens of identical copies of the dailies had to be made on VHS tapes for Montage.

- **The quality of the image** varied from poor to adequate. The quality of the EditDroid and other systems that used laserdisc media was very good, but complicated to obtain. The quality of the Montage image was equivalent to standard VHS tapes of the period, and not adequate for certain kinds of material. The image quality of the early Avids was poor compared to film (3,000 times less resolution). To store the image in a reasonable amount of disk space, it had to be rather crudely digitized, which resulted in a "pointillistic" effect that obscured detail and made it impossible to see hidden problems, such as lack of focus (which was also a problem with the Montage).

  This lack of screen resolution, to give an example, would encourage the editor to make more use of close-ups than was necessary. The determining factor for selecting a particular shot is frequently whether you can perceive the expression in the actor's eyes. If not, the editor will tend to use a closer shot, even though the longer shot is more than adequate when seen on the big screen. This of course affects the creative flow of the film.

- **Actual ease of making the cut itself**—being "user-friendly" at the ergonomic level: Some of the systems (Avid, for instance) were keyboard-intensive, which was not what most film editors were comfortable with. There needed to be an easy and immediate kinetic feedback between the material and the editor's eye-hand co-ordination, both in terms of selecting the desired frame and making the "splice" itself. Editing is a kind of frozen dance that depends on engaging as much of the editor's body as possible. EditDroid, based on the Steenbeck model, had the most "film-like" control.

- **"Works best when needed least."** Frequently, when called upon to perform a series of fast picture cuts or complicated sound edits, the tape and laserdisc systems would tell you in one way or another that you had overloaded their processing ability, and they could no longer show you your work in real time. Solving this was (and remains) simply a question of adding enough memory and processing speed to do the job.
- **Reliability of the edit decision list:** The reliability of the crucial edit decision list, from which the film is conformed to match what is in the computer, was problematic on the early systems.

  In Europe, where both film and video run at 25 frames a second, this is not a problem. But in the United States, motion-picture film runs at 24 frames per second and video runs at 30 frames, so a mathematical compatibility has to be worked out if the two systems are to mesh. In making copies of film to video, six extra "phantom" video frames (actually repetitions of existing frame-fields) are added every second.

> The early video-based electronic systems all ran at 30 frames per second, so there were times when the editor had decided to make a cut on a "phantom" video frame that had no numerical equivalent in film. The computer then had to make an arbitrary decision about which "real" frame to select: the one before or the one after the phantom frame. If only one version of the film was ever made, this would have been easier to resolve. But in the process of editing a film, changes upon changes upon changes are made, so the computer's decision to come down on the "left" side of a particular cut for the first version of the film might be followed by a decision to come down on the "right" side of the same cut in the second version—even if the editor had made no change in that area.
>
> On *Godfather III,* which was edited on the Montage system in 1990, we had to assign an assistant to manually double-check the edit decision list with what was actually on the editor's screen, and to cancel out edits of one frame that in fact had not been made at all.

This list above is not complete, but it gives a pretty good indication of the major electronic-editing issues that were foremost on editors' minds in the early 1990s. It was enough to dissuade many editors from taking the plunge and "going electronic." The advantages just didn't seem worth the potential troubles, and there were legendary stories of productions that had gotten hopelessly mired in electronic swamps, unable to extricate themselves except by returning to the old mechanical system.

This is a good place to pause and summarize what was a fairly chaotic situation, with very different systems in competition with each other: Moviola vs. KEM vs. EditDroid vs. Avid vs. Montage vs. Lightworks, etc.

It's important to realize that each system can be defined by three independent criteria:

1) Operation, which can be either mechanical or electronic
2) Storage of Media, which is either analog or digital
3) Access to Media, which is either random or linear.

The Moviola, for instance, is a random-access machine, even though it was invented in the 1920s. It would be fully defined as an MAR: Mechanical-Analog-Random. The Avid would be an EDR (Electronic-Digital-Random), the KEM would be an MAL (Mechanical-Analog-Linear), and so on.

Here is a table that summarizes all the variables:

		Operation		Storage of Media		Access to Media	
Machine	Decade	Mechanical	Electronic	Analog	Digital	Linear	Random
Moviola	'20s	M		A			R
KEM & Steenbeck	'30s	M		A		L	
EditDroid & Montage	'80s		E	A			R
Avid & Lightworks	'90s		E		D		R

One-and-a-Half English Patients

In 1995, I was hired to edit Anthony Minghella's film of Michael Ondaatje's *The English Patient.*

By this time, many of the problems outlined above had been solved—or were on their way to being solved—by the inexorable increase in processing speed of computers and a drop in the cost of memory. Although I had not edited a complete feature film electronically, I had directed and edited a four-minute music video for Linda Ronstadt in 1994, and a three-minute-long, five-layer newspaper montage for the film *I Love Trouble*, in 1995, both on the Avid. I was impressed by how things had changed in five years.

There had been three major breakthroughs:

1) **Memory capacity and processing speed** had increased to the point where storing the entire film on computer hard drives was now economically and technically possible; the quality of the digitized image had improved considerably; and the workflow was rarely interrupted.

2) **Two or more workstations** could now access the same set of hard drives on which the film was stored, which eliminated the danger of "bottlenecking."

3) **The software for a true 24-frame environment** had been written by Avid for their Film Composer program, assuring a one-to-one correspondence between the frames in the computer and the frames of film. This

was the breakthrough that made the crucial *edit decision list* perfectly reliable for the purposes of conforming the 35mm film.

Despite having a few lingering questions and reservations, I was eager to try digital editing, and *English Patient*, with its shifting time structure, seemed ideally suited for the flexibility that the Avid would give.

However, the producer of the film, Saul Zaentz, was trying to reduce the budget (all heads of departments were working on partial salary deferments), and renting an Avid represented an up-front extra cost of several thousand dollars a week—despite the potential for time savings farther along in the schedule. Also, *English Patient* was shooting in Italy and Tunisia, and Saul was rightly concerned about logistical support.

Anthony Minghella had edited his two previous films conventionally, on film, and was concerned about making the change to digital. Not only was it unfamiliar territory for him, but several of his friends had recently had unfortunate experiences with electronic editing: There had been technical problems, and the electronic system itself seemed to encourage studio interference.

So the decision was made to edit *The English Patient* directly on 35mm film, which was fine with me. Perhaps, on second thought, making a film in a foreign country and learning a new system at the same time would impose too many variables. There was always the next film . . .

So we started production of *English Patient* at Cinecittà in Rome in September of 1995 with a conventional mechanical setup: a KEM "8-plate" for me and a Steenbeck for my assistants, Daniel Farrell and Rosmary Conte, in addition to the normal rewind benches and miscellaneous paraphernalia. As usual, we had my computerized database to keep a log of the notes and comments about each take as well as the photo duplicating equipment for taking representative stills of each setup.

However, six weeks into production, my wife, Aggie (who was preparing to fly to Rome for a visit) called with the news that our son Walter, had had a seizure the day before and been diagnosed with a brain tumor.

I notified Anthony and Saul and discussed the situation with them as best I understood it—Walter was okay and recovering from the seizure, but an operation to remove the tumor had been tentatively scheduled for two weeks later. The seriousness of the situation couldn't be assessed until the day of the operation, when a biopsy could be made.

I told Anthony and Saul that I was flying home the next day, expected to be gone for at least eight weeks under the best of circumstances, and that they should think about hiring another editor to replace me. Both Saul and Anthony refused to consider that possibility and told me that I should not worry about the film and to update them. So early the next day I was on my way home to Bolinas, a small town north of San Francisco.

This kind of extreme crisis, for which you are never prepared, has the effect of hurtling you, so to speak, through the windshield of your normal day-to-day life. Some magic agency puts things, blessedly, in a startlingly clear perspective: What is important stands out in brilliant relief; everything else recedes into the muted background. The event-horizon shrinks to what is achievable today or at most tomorrow. "What if?" is banished, and your role in the unfolding events has a solidly determined feel. It's some kind of self-protective mechanism with very ancient roots.

So the film, which had been my primary focus twenty-four hours earlier, now seemed as if it were a curiosity at the other end of a telescope.

Nonetheless, I was conscious that I had a professional responsibility to people who had put their trust in me. I was going to be away for at least two months, and shooting was not going to stop: An eight-week backlog in a twenty-week schedule has a tremendous force to it.

By the time I landed in San Francisco, it had become clear to me what I would propose to Saul and Anthony: If they really wanted me to continue as the editor on the film, we should install an Avid in the barn next to our house in Bolinas, ship the dailies to San Francisco after the unit had seen them, and I would start editing at home, able to be close at hand during my son's recuperation. It would involve a considerable extra cost to the film, as well as having the editor 7,000 miles away from the production, but there didn't seem to be an alternative as far as I was concerned. To Saul and Anthony's eternal credit, they accepted my proposal without hesitation.

Walter's operation went ahead as scheduled, and was successful. The tumor's biopsy was ambiguous, and he declined to have chemotherapy or radiation treatment. He spent several months at home, through the first assembly of the film. The joke went around that, since my wife is English, we had one-and-a-half "English patients" staying with us at our house in Bolinas.

Walter had been teaching mountain-climbing before all this happened, and his recovery goal became being able to join a cancer survivor's ascent of Mt. Denali (we called it "Mt. Denial") in Alaska, the tallest peak in North America. In June of the following year, he was part of a team of fifteen that successfully reached the summit. He has now worked with me on my last three editing projects—it has been almost five years since the operation, and his prognosis is good, thank God.

Man Meets Machine

The Avid—which is physically just a powerful personal computer and some video monitors—was quickly installed upstairs in the barn, and film began to arrive from Italy. One problem was maintaining communication with my film assistants, Dan and Rosmary in Rome, as well as with Anthony and Saul, who were shooting in a remote part of Tunisia by this time. Luckily, Rosmary had an email account, and this quickly became the highway on which both correspondence and database information was transmitted.

And then there was the considerable puzzle of how to integrate the hour of material I had already cut on film into the new system, while moving forward on all other fronts. I don't know of another case of a film making this transition from mechanical to electronic in the middle of production, but the particular circumstances in this case demanded it. All the credit for making it as smooth as possible should go to my assistants: Edie Bleiman and Sean Cullen in San Francisco and Daniel Farrell and Rosmary Conte in Rome.

On videotape, the entire sixty hours of workprint for *English Patient* filled a couple of shelves of a medium-sized bookcase, and once Edie began to digitize it onto the hard drives, I found myself editing again—exactly two months after Walter's seizure.

Here I was, at home, with everything that I had asked for. The dilemma now: whether it all would go the way I had so hopefully predicted. How would my particular style of editing, developed on Moviolas and KEM, actually fare now that I had this mountain of backlogged material to get through on the Avid?

The first thing that pleased me was how easily the Avid adapted to my method of editing while standing up. With the KEM, it took at least three of us to lift an extremely heavy machine up onto reinforced plywood boxes. With the Avid, I simply placed the monitors on the top shelf of a metal storage rack, at eye level, and then pushed an inexpensive adjustable architect's table up against the rack. This setup gave me not only a place for the keyboard and mouse, but for spreading out up to eight pages of notes in front of me and right below the images—something I could never achieve with the mechanical systems. (By some good fortune, eight pages of notes turned out to be just the right number for even a fairly complicated scene.)

I was more than a little dismayed, however, by how degraded the image actually was, relative to film. To save money on storage, I had decided to digitize *English Patient* at resolution 4, which yields a relatively crude image. As I spent my first few days working with this resolution, however, I wondered if I had made a mistake, and whether I should now re-digitize at a higher resolution. Fortunately, while going over some paperwork on the third day, I happened to catch a glimpse of a still frame of Juliette Binoche on the monitor. It was so beautiful, in a kind of painterly, impressionistic way, that I felt more comfortable with my decision. "This is not the film," I told myself. "I am working on an impressionist painting of the film." Only time would tell whether this was a kind of whistling in the dark, but it gave me the courage to continue as planned.

I was buoyed somewhat in all this because my panels of still photographs (selected frames) from whichever scene I was working on were just to the right of the Avid console. These images, photographically taken directly from the workprint, served as a constant reminder of the true value of the images.

As for the Avid's actual operation, I was very happy to find that my old system of always cutting "in real time" (i.e., selecting the crucial last frame of a shot by marking it "on the fly" while the film is running at 24 frames per second) was actually easier on the Avid than it had been on the KEM or Moviola.

After a first attempt at selecting the "out" frame, the Avid would tell me, on my subsequent tries, how many frames I was late, or early, or whether (hopefully) I had hit the exact same frame. This was extremely valuable because it immediately quantified a feeling about what had happened on that second try. For instance, I might sense that I had cut a little too early, and a glance at the display would tell me that I was early by, say, three frames. So, under these circumstances, with this particular material, I would know what being "three frames early" felt like. This would make subsequent attempts that much easier and increasingly precise.

Mechanical systems provide this feedback, although in a slightly more involved way (I developed this approach while using mechanical systems), so I was greatly relieved to find that the Avid supplied this feature—and more quickly and automatically than on a mechanical system. I can't stress enough the importance of such immediate feedback: It's crucially important in the development of, and feeling for, the rhythmic signature of each particular film.

I also found that another of my editing peculiarities—making the first assembly of a scene without sound—was much easier on the Avid. With the Moviola or KEM, I could of course make a silent assembly easily enough (in fact, one of the reasons for excluding sound was to make a first assembly as quickly as possible), but hearing it would then involve a somewhat tedious couple of hours finding the correct sound tracks and synching them up to the picture by code number. In the Avid, the sound for the film is always running in synch with the image, so choosing to hear it or not is as simple as hitting a switch on or off.

I was initially suspicious of using the Avid's keyboard instead of the more-intuitive controls of the mechanical devices. The Moviola's design is almost automotive: It has pedals for forward and reverse motion and a hand brake that gives a particularly satisfying jolt when stopping the film. You can also grab hold of a fast-spinning flywheel with your left hand for additional braking power, and use it for inching the film forward or backward frame by frame. It is a tactile, whole-body experience in the extreme.

In other words, exactly what the Avid keyboard is not.

So I was amazed to find that, for me, this proved not to be an obstacle—I was even comfortable using my left hand to hit the crucial "cut" command. How quickly I adapted to the Avid's keyboard control is still a little mystifying. Perhaps I'm simply at ease with the keyboard in other situations. It may also be that my habit of editing standing up restores at least some of the Moviola's whole-body experience.

I also quickly came to appreciate two of the Avid's other features:

1) Its generous ability to manipulate multiple sound tracks synchronously with the picture, so that even at an early stage I could experiment with adding music and sound effects or multiple layers of dialogue. I was

also able to adjust and then establish the relative levels and equalizations of the sounds, something that would be impossible in the mechanical systems.

2) The provision of a large third monitor, separate from the Avid console's two "working" screens. I placed this to the side and across the room, so that I had to rotate ninety degrees to see it. Shifting my physical relationship to the images frequently helped me to see things in a different way.

I don't want to paint too rosy a picture—there were problems, of course. Some of them were trivial, some of them more serious and "interesting" (which I will get to in a minute). However, the Avid's advantages outweighed its disadvantages to the extent that I felt comfortable, confident, and excited to be working in this new environment. Even at such an early stage, the Avid roughly doubled the amount of film I was able to assemble every week. With the help of Pat Jackson, who came on as an associate editor for a month, in eight weeks we were able to catch up with the backlog of unedited film and have the four-and-a-half-hour first assembly of *English Patient* completed three weeks after the end of photography. This would not have been possible editing mechanically, and certainly not something that could be done easily at one's home. For that alone, if you know how long editors' days can be, I am grateful to digital editing.

(As a side note, after all the turbulence and uncertainty that we went through during this period, *The English Patient* went on to win nine Oscars, one of them for editing. In fact, it became the first digitally edited film to win an Oscar for editing.)

All the advantages of digital editing can give an intoxicating sense of freedom, particularly to editors who have been filing trims and rewinding reels for many years. But that sudden rush of freedom can be deceiving. As with every tool, the features of digital editing can cut both ways, and some of its most admired qualities have hidden, dark sides that can hurt if you are not aware of them in advance.

Let me explain what I mean with a few examples.

Random Access and Speed

One of the things I have not yet solved with digital editing, ironically, is how to deal most effectively with its central advantage—instant random-access.

Computerized editing systems achieve most of their speed by retrieving the requested material instantaneously, which is what we mean by "instant random-access." This allows the editor to do such things as effortlessly compare line readings from different takes. But random-access ultimately depends on knowing exactly what you want… and that is not always the case, as any editor can tell you.

The Moviola was a random-access machine, just not an *instant* random-access machine (unlike the KEM and Steenbeks, which are *linear*-access machines). Random-access systems are highly dependent on the quality of the notes made at the material's first viewing, because those notes are the key to unlocking and searching the vast library of material for each film. They necessarily reflect not only the note-taker's initial opinions about the material but also about the film itself, *as it is conceived at that time.*

As the film evolves, however, its needs change, and those original opinions may become outdated: A shot that was considered use*less* may thus become use*ful.* But unless there is a way of constantly re-examining the material, questioning those original assumptions, some useful material may remain buried forever under the original epitaph "No Good." The greater the amount of material, the more true this is. I have mentioned this aspect before, but it bears repeating in the present context. This constant review was a crucial part of the mechanical and creative process for me on linear machines (Steenbecks and KEM), which store the workprint in ten-minute rolls.

The human imagination is able to recognize ideas more powerfully than we can articulate them. When you are in a foreign country, you can always understand more of the language than you can speak. To a certain extent, every film that you make is a foreign country, and first you have to learn the language of that "country." Every film has (or should have) a unique way of communicating, and so you struggle to learn its language. But the film can speak its own language better than you can! So, in the mechanical, linear search for what I *wanted,* I would find instead what I *needed*—something different, better, more quirky, more accidental, more "true" than my first impression. I could recognize it when I saw it, but I couldn't have articulated it in advance. Picasso used to say, "I do not seek, I find"—which is another way of getting at the same idea.

The big selling point of any non-linear system, however, is precisely its non-linearity. "Get instantly where you want to go. All you have to do is tell the machine and it will give it to you instantly, like the perfect assistant." Yes, true enough, but that's actually something of a drawback because the machine gives me *only* what I ask for, and I don't always *want* to go where I *say* I want to go. Wanting something just gives me the starting point. I expect the material itself to tell me what to do next.

Now, technically, nothing prevents you from using the Avid as a linear machine—you can organize the material in large blocks and scroll at high speed through them just like on a KEM. But it's so easy to use random-access that, by default, it rules your decisions. How do you control your impulse to be immediately satisfied? I want what I want, so the machine—like the genie in the lamp—gives it to me. But something has been lost. Oscar Wilde's ironic observation applies here: "When God wants to punish somebody, He gives them what they want."

I should add that there's a subtle but profound difference in how film and digital move at high speed. On linear film machines, like the KEM, you achieve ten times normal speed by *reducing the amount of time* that any one frame is seen by ninety percent. So a frame is on for 1/240 of a second, not 1/24 of a second. It's very fast, but it's still there—you can still catch a little something from every single frame. But by the nature of their design, digital systems can't do that. They achieve ten times normal speed at the cost of *suppressing* ninety percent of the information. So if you ask a digital machine to go ten times faster than normal, it will do so by showing you only one frame out of every ten. It's like skipping a rock across the surface of a lake. You are *not seeing* ninety percent of the film—whereas when you watch sprocketed film at high speed on a KEM or Steenbeck, you see *everything*. I'm always amazed at how perceptive the human eye is, even at those high speeds, at detecting tiny inflections of looks and expression and action.

Maybe this is the reason that I have resisted using Avids as linear systems. Technically, I think this is a profound problem, something built into the nature of video monitoring: It takes an exact and unchangeable amount of time to scan a frame in video, and things can't go any faster than they do. Whereas on the KEM it's easy to increase the scan rate by simply speeding up the rotation of the prism in the lens.

The real issue with speed, though, is not just *how fast you can go*, but *where are you going so fast?* It doesn't help to arrive quickly if you wind up in the wrong place. And if arriving at your destination also produces a more complete knowledge of the material, the linear systems do have a serious advantage to offer.

Ultimately, however, technology is hardly ever the final determining factor in questions of speed vs. creativity. Here we are in the domain of the human spirit: what do you want to say and how do you want to say it? One hundred eighty years ago, Balzac wrote eighty classic novels in twenty years, using just a quill pen. Who among our word-processing writers today can even approach such a record? In the 1930s, Jean Renoir made a commercially successful feature film (*On Purge Bébé*) in three weeks—from concept to finished product. And early in his career, Kurosawa—directing and editing himself—would have the first cut of his films done two days after shooting.

Instead of "speed" digital systems would be more honest to advertise "increased options." They will allow the work to remain flexible longer, which is to say that the moment of decisive commitment can be delayed. This can have creative advantages, but it also can get you into trouble. In the 1930s, you had to plan out your shots very carefully when the Technicolor three-strip camera weighed half a ton. With lightweight cameras, fast film, and DAT or portable disk recorders, you can change your mind up to the last instant. Does it all happen faster? Not necessarily. A level of complexity is frequently added, which eats up the time gained. Is it better? That is arguable. The high-water mark of the American film industry is still recognized by many as 1939.

Using the right technology in the right way for your particular project centers on finding the correct balance of pre-planning vs. spontaneity—supporting structure vs. seductive surface. The human body is made up of flesh and bone and needs the right proportion of both to function the way it should.

- **Fewer assistants:** This may be achieved someday, when 35mm film is no longer used for photography and exhibition. But at present, movies that are edited digitally have in practice required *more* assistants, because there have to be people to handle the conforming of 35mm workprint as well as helping with the telecine, logging, and database work required by the hybrid process of working in a 35mm/digital world. This kind of crew tends to stratify along film/video lines and produce a subtle alienation—which is not ultimately good for the film, the people involved, or even the industry as a whole.

Arguably, the greatest period of creativity in European painting occurred at a time when painters required assistants to prepare their pigments and canvasses. All of the great painters of the Renaissance started out as assistants to established artists—there were no schools as such—and moved up the ladder, starting to help with the actual painting at a certain stage, until they were ready to work on their own, with their own assistants.

Not only did this provide real "on-site" training, free from the fog of theory that can settle over academic situations, but I'm sure that the presence of other people during the act of creation kept painting grounded in a way that it is obviously not today, when it's done almost exclusively in isolation. I can't count the number of times that feedback from my assistants has kept me honest about what worked or didn't work. They are my first audience. And many times they have provided the film with ideas beyond what I could have thought up myself.

The ultimate aim of computerized editing, however, is "one man/one machine"—an editor working as a painter works, alone in a room with all the material at his fingertips and no need for anyone around to help. If this level of isolation is ever achieved technically, it will be interesting to see the films that result, and to discover whether the collaboration that is the essence of filmmaking is not in some way compromised by this technical advance.

- **Reduced bookkeeping:** This is an area where computers shine. Electronic systems unquestionably gain a significant advantage by eliminating the filing of film trims—something that on an average feature would become the full-time occupation of at least one assistant. For most lower-budget films willing to take the risks involved with entirely eliminating workprint conformation, there is a real savings to be made.

  On the other hand, for higher-budget films that are obliged to screen different versions in 35mm, the need to conform the film and keep it up to date with the current version in the computer will involve all of the traditional mechanical bookkeeping and filing of trims and lifts in addition to database management for the computer.

  Another related advantage of digital systems is the ability of their databases to effortlessly archive different versions of the film for future reference. This, however, can be a slightly more dubious asset because it has the potential to open up a "sorcerer's apprentice" proliferation of information that may ultimately overwhelm the very goals it is trying to achieve.

Editing is (or should be) progressive—you are moving forward all the time. Even if you return to a previous structure, it will not be (or should not be) exactly as it was, but reflect in subtle ways what has happened to the film as a whole since the scene was first put together. By obsessively keeping every version of a scene, you can easily drown in all the variations, feeling some obligation to look at each of them and incorporate a little of each in subsequent versions. The result is that you may lose time and artistic focus in unproductive discussion, and the resulting work may have a stitched-together, Frankenstein's-monster feel to it rather than being organically whole and alive.

The key here is moderation. Restrict yourself to archiving significantly different versions of your film every two or three weeks. (Note that this archiving is different from the routine "backing up" of your work, which is an invisible background process that should be done on a daily basis in case of computer failure.)

- **No rewinding:** With random-access systems, no time is lost going back to the head of a sequence once you have arrived at the end. This is another advantage that has a "shadow" side, since (as we discussed earlier) digital systems subtract information at higher-than-normal speeds. Particularly when playing in reverse, digital systems do this subtracting in a random pattern that doesn't accurately reflect the rhythm of the editing. On an Avid, the only accurate way to look at your film is at normal speed, forward. Since this is how the film is going to be seen by an audience, why would it need to be seen any other way? For the same reason that painters will frequently look at their work in a mirror, upside down: By inverting the image, it is momentarily freed of content and can be looked at as pure structure. Driven by similar impulses, Catalonian architect Antonio Gaudí would build the models for his structures upside down, hanging them by wires so that he could immediately see the effect of an imbalance.

In the course of assembling a sequence on the KEM, I would naturally and frequently fast-rewind the 35mm film while it was still threaded through the prism. Something in the pure alternation of shapes and colors, seen out of the corner of my eye at high-speed reverse, told me something about the structure of the material that I couldn't have learned by looking at it "straight on" at normal-speed forward. But until I saw that true "backwardness" had disappeared from digital editing, I didn't really appreciate the unique virtues of reviewing-while-rewinding. You don't appreciate these kinds of things until they're gone.

- **Easier access:** On the face of it, this should be a good thing, and easier access participates in the general drift of technological innovation over the last forty years. Consumers of electronic hardware can now purchase devices that were closely guarded professional secrets as little as ten years ago. This has been particularly true in sound: The average car stereo system of the 1990s produced better sound than the most advanced recording studio of the 1950s. Computer customers today can buy relatively inexpensive editorial systems for their digital home videos that professionals would have envied ten years ago.

The hard truth, though, is that easier access does not automatically make for better results. The accompanying sense that "anyone can do it" can easily produce a broth spoiled by too many cooks. All of us today are able to walk into an art store and buy inexpensive pigments and supplies that the Renaissance painters would have paid fortunes for. And yet, do any of us paint on their level today?

On a more political note, once a film's workprint is digitized, only a few hours' work is needed to create an exact clone and establish another editing setup under the control of someone other than the director. In the days of mechanical editing, this would have been far too costly and time-consuming (and public) an option to even be contemplated. So-called digital "ghost cuts" are already being undertaken by some studios, and no one yet knows what the practical and creative long-term consequences will be.

On the bright side of that same coin, after a film has been completed, the uncut digitized images and sounds might be made available to film schools. This would allow editing students to practice their craft with "real-world" material that was professionally directed, shot, and recorded. Students would be able to examine in detail the problems that the filmmakers overcame, and perhaps find original solutions for themselves. They would then be able to compare their work to the professionally finished product.

- **A more civilized working environment:** Many years ago, I saw an advertisement for an interior-decorating firm that showed a split-level Park Avenue apartment featuring a beautiful Steinway Grand placed in the foreground. The text underneath asked us to "think of the music that Beethoven could have written if he had lived here!"

  The physicality of the Moviola would have certainly repelled the designers of that ad, and they would have applauded the look of the computer-editing suite in comparison. But is physicality really a bad thing? What kind of music *would* Beethoven have written in that apartment? And what would those interior decorators have thought of Rodin's sculpture studio? The most that can be said of the creative working environment is that it is probably a question of balance, like many things: comfortable, but not too comfortable; organized, but not too organized.

A film's editing room can be a place of considerable creative and political tension, and one of the mechanical systems "hidden" virtues is that their very physicality required you to move around a lot—certainly in comparison to working on a computer in front of a video screen. This could serve as a natural and unconscious means of releasing that tension.

Although the flatbed systems are more physical than the computer, they in turn require less physical movement than the Moviola. When I first started using a Steenbeck, I developed what I called "Steenbeck neck"—a tension in the upper shoulders that came from sitting at the Steenbeck and only having to move my fingers and wrists to edit. To combat this, I raised my KEM, and now my Avid, fifteen inches higher than normal so that I work standing up, as I had done with the Moviola.

I can sit whenever I want (I have an architect's chair), but most of the time, and especially at the decisive moment of making a cut, I will always be on my feet. I want to be able to stand and react as quickly as possible—like a gunslinger—and having your whole body engaged in the process helps immeasurably.

Digital Editing—Faster, Faster, Faster?

One of the most frequently asked questions about digital editing is, "Are movies getting faster? Do films have more quick cuts simply because it's *digital* and they *can* be cut faster?" Well, that's true as far as it goes—it's easier to cut quickly on digital machines because you have random-access and don't have to make all those physical splices and file away all those trims.

But as a general trend over the last fifty years, the editing pace of films has been increasing. This is probably due to the influence of television commercials, which have accustomed us to a visual shorthand that was developed to pack more information into expensive time slots and to attract and hold the eye in an environment—the home—where there is much competition for that attention.

Sunset Boulevard (1950), for instance, has a rate of eighty-five cuts in the first twenty minutes, which is typical for its time and about half of today's average. The opening twenty minutes of *The Sixth Sense* (1999) has exactly double that number of cuts—170. And the final twenty minutes of *Fight Club* (1999) has more than double again—375.

However, there are exceptions to this historical trend: *The Third Man,* made in 1949, has a beautifully effective rapid style of 225 cuts in the first twenty minutes. That pace is right for *Third Man*, which is scripted and directed to accommodate and exploit such *brio* (compare the words-per-minute rate of narration for *Sunset* with the rapid-fire narration for *Third Man),* just as certain pieces of music are written and orchestrated to be played quickly. There is no "right" or "wrong" speed, obviously. Problems arise when you have something that was written *largo* played *prestissimo,* or vice versa.

What was implicit in the question about quick cutting was the feeling that maybe films were now *too* quickly cut, and that perhaps some blame could be laid at the door of digital editing.

I have heard directors say that they were disappointed when they finally saw their digitally edited films projected on a big screen. They felt that the editing now seemed "choppy," though it had seemed fine on the television monitor. These directors had to go back, undo everything, and start again. They felt betrayed, and blamed it somehow on "digital."

The editor has some immediate control over two perceptual issues in the editing room: the amount of detail that is visible in the image and the size of the image itself. Both of these can affect the rhythm of the film.

- **Detail** is an issue particularly relevant to digital editing because the film has to be digitally compressed to get it to fit economically on the hard drive of the computer, and this can significantly reduce the amount of visual information in any frame. As a result, there may be so little detail that the eye can absorb all of it very quickly, leading the careless editor to cut sooner than if he had been looking at the fully detailed film image.

  When the 35mm film is conformed and projected, however, that latent richness suddenly blossoms, and the eye now feels that the images are following each other too quickly to fully absorb all that is there—hence the choppiness that the directors complained about.

What steps can be taken to avoid this problem?

First, be aware that *image detail* and *pace* are intimately related.

Second, digitize at the highest resolution that your production can afford, so that you get the most detail possible on your screen.

Third, print and screen 35mm workprint dailies, if your production can afford it. Once you've seen the detail in a shot, it's harder to forget later on.

Fourth, conform the 35mm workprint to the version in the computer as soon as possible, keep it up to date regularly, and have 35mm screenings of your film as often as possible.

I realize that for many low-budget films it's unrealistic to be able to do all four, but your film will be better the more of them you can accomplish.

As a consolation, the detail in digitized images has improved tremendously in the last ten years. As long as computers' efficiency and speed keep increasing as they have (a dollar today buys 400 times the storage capacity of ten years ago), I expect this to disappear as an issue within a short time.

- **Image size** is an issue closely related to image detail, but is not unique to digital editing. How do you deal with the disparity between the small image in the cutting room (on a Moviola, KEM, or Avid) and the huge image that will be shown in theaters? It is the difference between painting a miniature and a mural. With a small screen, your eye can easily take in everything at once, whereas on a big screen it can only take in sections at a time. You tend to look *at* a small screen, but *into* a big screen. If you are looking *at* an image, taking it all in at once, your tendency will be to cut away to the next shot sooner.

With a theatrical film, particularly one in which the audience is fully engaged, the screen is not a surface, it is a magic window, sort of a looking glass through which your whole body passes and becomes engaged *in* the action *with* the characters on the screen. If you really like a film, you're not aware that you are sitting in the cinema watching a movie. Your responses are very different than they would be with television.

Television is a "look-at" medium, while cinema is a "look-into" medium. You can think of the television screen as a surface that the eye hits and then bounces back. The trick with electronic editing, of course, is that since you are watching television monitors, you must somehow convince yourself that these are cinematic screens: You must make "look at" become "look into."

One of the functions of music videos and commercials is to attract your attention and keep it. While watching television, you're usually looking at a small screen some distance away for a short period of time. Visual competition is all around: The lights are on, the phone may be ringing, you might be in a supermarket or department store. Television has to make things collide within that tiny frame in order to catch your attention because of the much narrower angle that the image subtends compared to theatrical film—hence the quick cuts, jump cuts, swish pans, staggered action, etc.

There's a completely different aesthetic when you're in a theater: The screen is huge, everything else in the room is dark, there are (hopefully) no distractions, you are there for at least two hours; you can't stop the film at your convenience. And so, understandably, feature editing has to be paced differently than music-video or commercial editing.

What can be done to help with this problem of size, the miniature vs. the mural?

First, as with image detail, be aware that the eye takes in a large picture differently, at a different rate, than a small one.

Second, conform the 35mm film and have as many screenings with as large a screen as your production can manage.

Third—and this is my own personal solution—cut out two little paper figures and place them on either side of the monitor screen, making them the correct size in relationship to the screen as real human beings will be when the film is finally projected in a theater. So, if I am looking at a twenty-two-inch-wide screen in the editing room, I will make my little people four-

and-a-half inches tall. This will make the monitor screen look, with a little imagination, as if it is thirty feet wide. Generally, I like this kind of solution because it's simple. You don't think it would amount to much, but this practice helps tremendously in solving problems before they occur.

Why don't we just edit in large rooms with big screens? Well, with digital editing and video projection, we could, very easily, be editing with a thirty-foot screen. The real estate for the room would be expensive, however. More expensive than my little paper leprechauns.

It would be an interesting experiment, however, to edit with a thirty-foot screen.

General Observations: The Celluloid Amazon

No matter what editing system you are using, you will always be confronting astronomical numbers of different possible versions. (Remember that mathematical formula with the "!" in it.) When those numbers were physically represented by mountains—tons—of actual film, you knew instinctively that you had to have a plan and be organized from the start. Contemplating the thicket of five hundred thousand or a million feet of dailies is like peering into the Amazon jungle. Who would go in there without a map and adequate supplies?

One of digital systems' dangers is that, superficially, they turn that Amazon jungle into a video game without apparent consequences. If you lose, you simply start over again from the beginning! No film has actually been touched! There are no loose ends to restitch together.

In a certain trivial sense, this is true, but it doesn't mean that a real Amazon isn't lurking behind the virtual one, with real consequences should you lose your way. There should always be planning, no matter what—you only have so much time. You can never explore all the possible versions—there should always be a map. Human memory has its limitations—you should always take detailed notes of what you've seen.

Theseus needed his thread to get out of the Minotaur's maze. With no plan, no map, no thread, film editing becomes just a thrashing about, a slamming together of images and sounds for momentary effect. But this kind of effect will have no long-term resonance with the film as a whole.

So, paradoxically, the hidden advantage of editing sprocketed film was that the weight and volume of it encouraged the editor to take things seriously and to plan ahead before jumping in—to develop certain strategies and defensive mechanisms. For me, this took the form of my "reverse storyboard" system of images and my database system of notation. All of us who have grown up as editors of sprocketed film were privileged to develop our own strategies for dealing with our own Amazons, and many of these strategies should not now be thoughtlessly discarded, but rather adapted to the digital age that is upon us.

The Digital Present

When regulated postal service was finally established in Great Britain and Royal Mail started to be carried on trains for the first time—somewhere around 1840—it unleashed a torrent of letter-writing among those who were able to do so. People routinely dashed off twenty-page letters three times a week to several correspondents simultaneously, not so much because they had anything particularly compelling to say to each other, but simply from the exhilaration of being able to say it—and have it reliably received across the country in a matter of days, rather than the unreliable weeks that it took in the days of coach and horses.

Something similar is happening today with the internet. In fact, any significant technological breakthrough will create a surge of exploratory interest that can only be satisfied by creating a pretext for the exploration. For a while, *what* is communicated is less important than *the means by which* it is communicated. Eventually, down the road, the new technology is assimilated and content re-establishes its primacy. We are somewhere along that road with computer-assisted editing, but since things are still evolving so rapidly it's hard to say exactly how far we have come. I sense that we have actually come a long way in a short time.

When I wrote the first edition of this book eight years ago, I felt that we would not know where we were until four milestones had been passed:

1) **Memory storage** had become more efficient by an order of magnitude, so that it's pos-

sible to store at least forty to one hundred hours of high-quality picture "on line," having it all equally accessible at all times.

2) **The cost** of a fully operational system capable of editing a feature drops well below $100,000, or into the range that you would expect to spend for a KEM.

3) **The creation** of the digital equivalent of the 35mm *sprocket/timecode* relationship: a universal standard that would operate across all the technical environments in which image and sound are manipulated, and which would provide an immutable point of reference for the picture/sound relationship.

4) **35mm film** is no longer shown theatrically. Release prints are replaced by a digital equivalent that is as good or better than 35mm film.

As of the year 2001, the first three of those milestones have now been passed, and the fourth—digital projection—is with us but not yet universal.

1) In 1994, it became possible, technically and economically, to store the entire digitized workprint of a feature film on hard disks that were simultaneously accessible to the editor and the editor's assistant.

   In 1999, *The Insider* stored 1,200,000 feet (222 hours) of workprint, the most that any film had digitized up to that point (coincidentally, the same amount of workprint as *Apocalypse Now*).

2) In 1996, an Avid system with two editorial work stations cost $160,000—or $80,000 a station—compared to the price of a KEM "8-plate," which was around $65,000.

   In 1999, *Any Given Sunday* had nine workstations (six editors and three assistants), all accessing the same set of hard drives.

3) In 1997, Open Media Framework software became available. OMF allows different sound and picture editing systems to "talk" to each other—a more sophisticated version of how the sprocket/timecode relationship allows different 35mm and tape systems to remain in synch with each other.

   A functioning OMF meant that on *The Talented Mr. Ripley,* the work that I did on the eight sound tracks in my Avid was exported to the ProTools workstations that were being used by Pat Jackson and her dialogue editors.

   As a result, all of the sound cuts, overlaps, level changes, fades and dissolves were reproduced exactly and applied to the sound in the hard drives of the ProTools systems, where they could be further refined.

   It is important to remember that, as with all computerized systems, the creative decisions about what to do with the sound are held in a separate place from the sound itself. Only the decisions are being exported from Avid to ProTools. The sound, uncut and unmanipulated, is present on the hard drives of both systems.

Prior to OMF, the selected sound would have to be reloaded in real time, and then the sound editors would have to recreate all of the cuts, fades, dissolves, etc., that had been made in the Avid. In effect, they would have to reinvent the wheel that had already been created.

4) In 1999, *Phantom Menace, Tarzan, An Ideal Husband,* and *Toy Story II* were all exhibited in digital projection in selected theaters in the United States and Europe.

The implications of this last development are perhaps the most profound of all. Thirty-five-millimeter film has been the physical and metaphorical foundation upon which the whole superstructure of motion pictures has been built. Its eventual elimination and replacement by a powerful, flexible, but elusive string of digits raises technical and artistic questions that will take many years to resolve.

The Digital Future

Sound editors have always thought in what I would call the vertical and horizontal dimensions at the same time. The sound editor naturally moves forward through the film in "horizontal" time—one sound follows another. But he also has to think vertically, which is to say, "What sounds are happening at the same time?" There might be, for example, the background sound of a freeway along with birds singing, a plane passing overhead, footsteps of pedestrians, etc. Each of these is a separate layer of sound, and the beauty of the sound editor's work, like a musician's, is the creation and integration of a multidimensional tapestry of sound.

Up until now, however, picture editors have thought almost exclusively in the horizontal direction: The question to be answered was simply, "What's next?" As you can tell from my math at the beginning, that's complicated enough—there are a tremendous number of options in the construction of a film. In the future, that number is going to become even more cosmic because film editors will have to start thinking vertically as well, which is to say: "What can I edit *within the frame*?"

Optical-effects work has become sophisticated and subtle, many times not even noticeable as an effect. This permits the director or editor to say, "I don't really like that sky after all" or "I think this should be winter, so let's get rid of the leaves in this shot." In the near future, machines such as the Avid, which are good at manipulation in the sequential horizontal dimension, will fuse with special-effects machines such as the Inferno, which are good at manipulation in the simultaneous vertical dimension. There will be some unforeseen consequences—can one editor actually handle all this? Or will the work be divided between two crews, a Vertical Team and a Horizontal Team?

In the old days, if you wanted to do a special effect, such as replacing the blue sky with another color, you had to use a special Vista-Vision or 70 mm camera to get a large-format negative so that the grain of multiple reprintings wouldn't show. Now, because of the accuracy of digital reproduction, none of that is an issue. A tremendous amount of time also used to be spent in shooting special effects—if somebody flew through the air, they were attached to cables. Consequently, the cameraman had to light the scene so that the cables would be as invisible as possible. Now, with digital effects, you make the cables big and brightly colored, because they then become easier to see and digitally remove.

The Holy Grail, of course, is an Avid/Inferno editing/effects machine that actually produces the final product, not just a sketch of the final product. To some extent, this has already been achieved in television, but not in features, where the resolution has to be correspondingly much higher for the big screen.

While we are at it, here are several predictions that will probably materialize in the near future, if they haven't already by the time this book comes out:

- **The end of magnetic film.** Revolutionary in its own way when it appeared around 1950, sprocketed magnetic sound film is already being displaced by removable drives running in synch with the projector. We used Jaz drives on *The Talented Mr. Ripley*. Each of these can be copied instantly and is capable of holding the information of forty reels of magnetic film, at a savings of more than 40:1.

- **Direct feed from the camera.** Some kind of beam-splitter device that will allow a digital disk recording to be made alongside the 35mm film. This disk recording will be delivered to the editor immediately, rather than waiting for the film to be developed and synched, screened, telecined, and digitized.

  This will be a temporary solution pending the development of all-digital cameras and the elimination of film as a recording medium.

- **Competition for the Avid.** At the moment, the Avid system is by far the most frequently used professional system, followed by Lightworks, which has had a difficult few years recently.

  Serious threats to Avid's dominance, however, are now coming from very inexpensive, almost "consumer-level" systems, such as Apple's Final Cut Pro, Adobe Premiere, EditDV, and Media 100. Final Cut Pro, for instance, is now commonly used for cable television features, yet its cost is one-twentieth of an Avid system.

  Until recently, these systems were unable to provide a reliable interface with 35mm negative, and so their use was practically limited to motion pictures whose final format was video. Third-party software, however, such as FilmLogic, has been invented to fill this gap, and Apple has recently acquired Focal Point Systems, the developers of FilmLogic, so Apple seems intent on competing directly with Avid.

It will be interesting to see Avid's response to these developments.

- **The final product.** The day will come when the editor is dealing with images of such resolution that they will be projectable in a theater. In effect, the output of the Avid will be the answer print. As I mentioned, this is already happening in television, and following Moore's Law (processing speed per unit of currency doubles every eighteen months), it's simply a matter of time before the hypothetical Avid/Inferno (or some equivalent machine) is capable of real-time manipulation of images with a resolution of 4,000 lines—the equivalent of 35mm film.

All of these projected developments point in roughly the same direction, toward an ever-more-integrated digital cinema. Early in this new millennium, we are still living in a hybrid world where sprocketed 35mm film plays an important role in production and exhibition. But I doubt that film will remain vital much longer. In some ways, the situation is similar to that of domestic lighting around the turn of the last century. In 1900, chandeliers were fitted for both gas and electricity. Electricity was new, it was exciting, it produced a brilliant light (what the French disapprovingly called a "fleshless flame"), but electricity was also expensive and not quite as dependable as it should have been. And so there would also be gas—romantic, dangerous, inefficient, "fleshy," but familiar and dependable.

For the moment, cinema is caught in a similar "double-chandelier" phase in which we have to deal with film as a sprocketed, photographic, material medium, and with the electronic image as a digital, virtual, immaterial medium. But just as surely as gaslight passed from our daily lives, sooner or later so will 35mm film.

What, then, are the technical and artistic implications of a completely digital cinema? Will it be its own kind of "fleshless flame" or something else? A difficult question, because we are right in the middle of furious change, but perhaps something can be learned from similar situations in the development of other forms of art. In fact...

Gesamtkunstkino—Total Art Cinema

...if only we could just stop that gentleman in the top hat coming out of the Metropolitan Opera—no, no, *him,* the one with the fur collar—and ask about the performance of *Tannhäuser* he has just attended. Perhaps, if he were agreeable, we could walk with him up Broadway and let the conversation go where it might, since this is December 1899, and one's thoughts are naturally turned toward the coming twentieth century.

What about the stunning production that he has just seen? Truly unbelievable! And perhaps a word about the future of opera—specifically Richard Wagner's concept of *Gesamtkunstwerk—Total Art Work,* the ultimate fusion of music, drama, and image? What wonders will audiences be seeing in a 100 years time?

As he stops to consider this last question, one can't help but glance over his shoulder at the sight of dozens of people in the shop behind him, mostly men, mostly young, mostly immigrants, with their heads plunged into some kind of mechanism, hands cranking madly away in a kind of trance. By chance, we have stopped in front of an amusement arcade, and the men inside are operating Kinetoscopes and watching images of young ladies disrobing over and over again before their very eyes.

As our fur-collared friend is excitedly anticipating a century of high culture and operatic triumphs to make those of the nineteenth century pale in comparison, we—time travelers who know the truth—can't help suppressing a smile. Imagine our new acquaintance's astonishment and repugnance at being told that the noisy and offensive contraptions behind him would shortly transform themselves into the dominant art form of the twentieth century and stage their own assault on the citadel of Total Art Work; and that although his beloved operas would still be performed in 1999, and lavishly, they would be—mostly—reworkings of the nineteenth century's preserved-in-amber canon, the West's own version of Japanese Kabuki.

Of course, we won't disappoint him with our insights, which would seem like typical ravings from the strange-looking creatures he usually takes pains to avoid. What is New York coming to these days? Good-bye, nice talking to you.

Without much warning, we are back in the New York of December, 1999. *Toy Story II* has recently opened, and the lines have not gotten any shorter. In fact, at one theater in Times Square they have gotten somewhat longer.

Strolling by the marquee, we discover why: *Toy Story II* is being projected digitally, without film. The sprocketed 35mm celluloid that serviced our friends at the amusement arcade in 1899 and the expanding cinematic dreams of the twentieth century—through the arrival of sound, color, wide-screen, three dimensions (for a few years, anyway), Dolby Stereo—the physical medium that carried all these inventions uncomplainingly on its shoulders is, at the end of the century, about to put down its burdens and slip away. In a few years, film will become a historical curiosity, like parchment or vellum.

And the three ubiquitous symbols for the motion picture—the reel, the clapstick, and film itself with those characteristic little square sprocket holes running down its edges—will all be anachronistic, referring to a forgotten technology, like the carpenter's adz and awl.

Is this something to be concerned about?

By way of comparison, Gutenberg's first Bible was printed on vellum, a beautiful and tactile organic substance, but printing only really took off with the invention of paper, which was cheap and easy to manufacture. Gutenberg's concept of movable type transcended the medium used for the printing itself. Digital, almost certainly, will prove to be paper to celluloid's parchment.

So let's declare confidently that although *film* may fade away, there will always be *pictures that move.* The insight that gave rise to motion pictures, Joseph Plateau's quantization of movement in the 1830s (extended to photography by Muybridge in the 1870s) is as profound in its way as Gutenberg's invention of printing in the 1450s, and just as independent of the medium of transmission.

As astonishing as it is to see digitally projected images—clear or clearer than 35mm film, with none of the scratches, dirt, or jitter that infects even the most pristine of 35mm prints—the truth is that for fifteen years, the film industry has been steadily turning digital from the inside out. The triumphs of digital visual effects, of course, were already well known before their apotheosis in *Jurassic Park, Titanic, Phantom Menace,* and *The Matrix.* But the arrival of digital projection will trigger the final capitulation of the two last holdouts of film's nineteenth-century mechanical-analog legacy. Projection, the end of the line, is one—the other is the original photography that begins the whole process. The current film industry is a digital sandwich between slices of analog bread.

Once digital projection makes significant inroads, however, film laboratories such as Technicolor will find it difficult to operate in the black, since most of their profits come from massive theatrical print orders, sometimes as high as 50,000,000 feet of film per motion picture. When (not if) the laboratories go out of the film business, motion-picture companies will inevitably turn to digital cameras for original photography. In the summer of 2000, George Lucas dispensed with film entirely and shot the next *Star Wars* film with Sony high-definition digital cameras.

In the almost-immediate future, then—when final projection *and* original photography are digitized—the entire technical process of filmmaking will be digital from start to finish, and the whole technical infrastructure will telescope in upon itself with great suddenness. Some of the consequences of this we can foresee; others are unpredictable. But this transformation will likely be complete in less than ten years.

Of course, there will be wonders to compensate us for the loss of our old friends Clapstick, Sprocket, and Reel. Of course, the blurring of borders between video, computers, and film will vastly increase. Of course, digital creatures (and perhaps even actors) will be born that will make 1993's *Jurassic Park* seem like 1933's *King Kong*. Of course, channel 648 will be a live transmission of the planet Earth as seen from the Moon, in stunning detail, occupying the entire liquid-crystal wall of your media room.

But what will *cinema*—the habit of seeing motion pictures in a theatrical setting—what will *cinema* be like in 2099?

Will the digital revolution, so intoxicatingly heady at the moment, transform cinema into something unrecognizable to us today, for better or worse?

Will cinema perhaps have ossified by 2099 into the twenty-first century's version of Grand Opera? Tuxedo-clad crowds attending yet another projection of 160-year-old *Casablanca,* unimaginably enhanced by some technological grandson of today's digital wizardry?

Or perhaps cinema will have disappeared completely, overrun by some technical-social upheaval as unimaginable to us as the Kinetoscope's ultimate transformation in 1899. The parallels between the immigrants cranking their Kinetographs in the amusement arcade and your teenager locked in his room with Lara Croft (from the Tomb Raider game) are striking.

Of course, as soon as we pose these questions, we know it's silly even to attempt an answer. But it is December 1999, after all—the end of a millennium. Why not?

Is the complete digitization of the art and industry of cinema something that will be ultimately good for it?

To even attempt an answer to a question like that, we need to find some analogous development in the past. The one that seems closest, to me, is the transformation in painting that took place in the fifteenth century, when the old technique of pigments on *fresco* was largely replaced by oil paint on canvas.

Some of the greatest, if not *the* greatest, triumphs of European pictorial art were done in fresco, the painstaking process whereby damp plaster is stained with various pigments that, as they dry, bond chemically with the plaster and change color. One need only think of Michelangelo's frescoed ceiling of the Sistine Chapel, the pictorial equivalent of Beethoven's Ninth Symphony.

A great deal of advance planning needs to be done with fresco. Its variables—such as the consistency and drying time of the plaster—have to be controlled exactly. The artists who worked in fresco needed a precise knowledge of the pigments and how they would change color as they dried. Once a pigment had been applied, no revisions were possible. Only so much work could be done in a day, before the plaster applied that morning became too dry. Inevitably, cracks would form at the joints between subsequent applications of plaster. The arrangement of each day's subject matter had to be chosen carefully to minimize the damage from this unpredictable cracking.

It should be clear that fresco painting was an expensive effort of many people and various interlocking technologies, overseen by the artist, who took responsibility for the final product.

The invention of oil paint changed all of this. The artist was freed to paint wherever and whenever he wanted. He did not have to create a work in its final location. His paint was the same color wet as it would eventually be when dry. He did not have to worry unduly about cracking surfaces. And the artist could paint over areas that he didn't like, even to the point of reusing canvasses for completely different purposes.

Although painting in oils remained collaborative for a while, the innate logic of the new medium encouraged the artist to take more and more control of every aspect of his work; intensifying his personal vision. This was tremendously liberating, and the history of art from 1450 to the present is a clear testimony to the creative power of that liberation—and some of its dangers, which found ultimate expression in the late nineteenth and twentieth centuries, with the emergence of solitary and tortured geniuses like Van Gogh.

The nature of working with film has been more like painting in fresco than oil. It's so heterogeneous, with so many technologies woven together in a complex and expensive fabric, that filmmaking is almost by definition impossible for a single person to control. There are a few solitary filmmakers—Jordan Belson comes to mind—but these are exceptional individuals, and their films' subject matters are geared to allow creation by a single person.

By contrast, digital techniques naturally *tend* to integrate with each other because of their mathematical commonality, and thus become easier to control by a single person. I can see this already happening in the sound-mixing work that I do, where the borders between sound editing and mixing have begun to blur. And this blurring is about to happen in the further integration of film editing and visual effects.

So let's suppose a technical apotheosis sometime in the middle of the twenty-first century, when it somehow becomes possible for a single person to make an entire feature film, with virtual actors. Would this be a good thing?

If the history of oil painting is any guide, the broadest answer would be yes, with the obvious caution to keep a wary eye on the destabilizing effect of following too intently a hermetically personal vision. One need only to look at the unraveling of painting or classical music in the twentieth century to see the risks.

Let's go even further, and force the issue to its ultimate conclusion by supposing the diabolical invention of a black box that could directly convert a single person's thoughts into a viewable cinematic reality. You would attach a series of electrodes to various points on your skull and simply *think* the film into existence.

And since we are time-traveling already, let us present this hypothetical invention as a Faustian bargain to the future filmmakers of the twenty-first century. If this box were offered to you by some mysterious cloaked figure in exchange for your eternal soul, would you take it?

The kind of filmmakers who would accept or even leap at the offer are driven by the desire to see their own vision on screen in as pure a form as possible. They accept present levels of collaboration as the necessary evil to achieve their visions. Alfred Hitchcock, I imagine, would be one of them, judging from his description of the creative process: "The film is already made in my head before we start shooting."

The kind of filmmakers who would instead reject the offer are interested foremost in the *collaborative process* of filmmaking, and in seeing a detailed vision mysteriously *emerge out of* that process, rather than being imposed by a single individual from the beginning. Francis Ford Coppola's colorful description of his role sums it up: "The director is the ringmaster of a circus that is inventing itself."

The paradox of cinema is that it is most effective when it seems to fuse two contradictory elements—

the general and the personal—into a kind of *mass intimacy*. The work itself is unchanging, aimed at an audience of millions, and yet—when it works—a film seems to speak to each member of the audience in a powerfully personal way.

The origins of this power are mysterious, but I believe they come from two of the primary characteristics of motion pictures: that it is a theater of thought and that it is a collaborative art.

Film is a dramatic construction in which, for the first time in history, characters can be *seen to think* at even the subtlest level, and these thoughts can then be choreographed. Sometimes these thoughts are almost physically visible, moving across the faces of talented actors like clouds across the sky. This is made possible by two techniques that lie at the foundation of cinema itself: the closeup, which renders such subtlety visible, and the cut—the sudden switch from one image to another—which mimics the acrobatic nature of thought itself.

And collaboration, which is not necessarily a compromise, may be the very thing, if properly encouraged, that allows film to speak in the most developed way to the largest number of people. Every person who works on a film brings his or her own perspective to bear on the subject. And if these perspectives are properly orchestrated by the director, the result will be a multi-faceted and yet integrated complexity that will have the greatest chance of catching and sustaining the interest of the audience, which is itself a multi-faceted entity in search of integration.

None of the foregoing, however, addresses the fact that cinema is, by definition, a theatrical, communal experience for the audience as well as the authors, but one in which the play remains the same each time it's shown. It is the audience's reactions that change.

The mid-twentieth century pessimism about the future of cinema, which foresaw a future ruled by television, overlooked the perennial human urge—at least as old as language itself—to leave the home and assemble in the fire-lit dark with like-minded strangers to listen to stories.

The cinematic experience is a recreation of this ancient practice of theatrical renewal and bonding in modern terms, except that the flames of the stone-age campfire have been replaced by the shifting images that are telling the story itself. Images that dance the same way every time the film is projected, but which kindle different dreams in the mind of each beholder. It is a fusion of the permanency of literature with the spontaneity of theater.

I would like to emphasize the words *leaving of familiar surroundings*. The theatrical/cinematic experience is really born the moment someone says, "Let's go out." What is implicit in this phrase is a dissatisfaction with one's familiar surroundings and the corresponding need to open oneself up in an uncontrolled way to something "other." And here we have the battle between *motion pictures in the home* and *cinema*, for I'll venture that the true cinematic experience can't be had in the home, no matter how technically advanced the equipment becomes.

I am struck, for example, at how often someone tells me that they have seen a certain film in a theater and that they were impressed with the level of detail in picture and sound, something they never experienced when they saw the same film on video at home.

Well, I have seen both the film and the video, and I have to say that, by and large, the level of detail is comparable, if not exactly the same. What is definitely not the same, however, is the state of mind of the viewer.

At home, you are king, and the television is your jester. If you are not amused, you take out the remote control and chop off his head! The framework of home viewing is familiarity: What is right is what fits with the routine, which implies a mind-set that sees only what it wants—or is prepared—to see.

Going out, however, involves some expense, inconvenience, and risk. Remember that you will be sitting in a dark room with as few as six, or as many as six hundred strangers—perhaps even more. No distractions, no way to stop the film once it starts, and it starts at a certain time whether or not you are there. This produces a mind set that is open to experience in a way that home viewing can never replicate. Most mysteriously important, however, are those six or six hundred strangers sitting with you, whose muffled presence alters and magnifies the nature of what you see in an unquantifiable way.

Let's say that the average age in the audience is twenty-five years. Six hundred times twenty-five equals fifteen thousand years of human experience assembled in that darkness—well over twice the length of recorded human history of hopes, dreams, disappointments, exultation, tragedy. All focused on the same series of images and sounds, all brought there by the urge, however inchoate, to open up and experience as intensely as possible something beyond their ordinary lives.

The new century has recently turned, the digital revolution has not swept the field (yet, anyway), and when it does, it will be many years before Mephistopheles arrives with his electrode-studded black box. There will be collaboration in motion pictures, grudging or not, for many years to come. But it seems that if we are looking out for the shadow that digital might cast, we might look in the direction of anything that encourages a solitary monolithic vision and discourages developed complexity—both at the beginning, in the production of film, and at the end, in its theatrical enjoyment.

And since I'm here to draw conclusions, I'll come down on the affirmative side and say that cinema *will* be with us a hundred years from now. Different of course, but still cinema. Its persistence will be fueled by the unchanging human need for stories in the dark, and its evolution will be sparked by the technical revolutions now getting under way. We are perhaps now where painting was in 1499. So we have a few good centuries ahead of us, if we are careful.

Beyond that, who knows? Let's meet again in 2099 and have another look around.

Walter Murch has been honored by both British and American Motion Picture Academies for his picture editing and sound mixing. In 1997, Murch received an unprecedented double Oscar for both film editing and sound mixing on *The English Patient* (1996, dir. A. Minghella), as well as the British Academy Award for best editing. Seventeen years earlier, he received an Oscar for best sound for *Apocalypse Now* (1979, dir. F. Coppola), as well as British and American Academy nominations for his picture editing on the same film. He also won a double British Academy Award for his film editing and sound mixing on *The Conversation* (1974, dir. F. Coppola), was nominated by both academies for best film editing for *Julia* (1977, dir. F. Zinnemann), and in 1991 received two Oscar nominations for Best Film Editing for the films *Ghost* (dir. J. Zucker) and *The Godfather, Part III* (dir. F. Coppola).

Among Murch's other picture editing credits are for *The Unbearable Lightness of Being* (1988, dir. P. Kaufman), *House of Cards* (1993, dir. Michael Lessac), *Romeo is Bleeding* (1994, dir. P. Medak), *First Knight* (1995, dir. J. Zucker), and *The Talented Mr. Ripley* (1999, dir. A. Minghella)

Murch was the re-recording mixer for *The Rainpeople* (1969, dir. F. Coppola), *THX-1138* (1971, dir. G. Lucas), *The Godfather* (1972, dir. F. Coppola), *American Graffiti* (1973, dir. G. Lucas), *The Godfather, Part II* (1974, dir. F. Coppola), and

Crumb (1994, dir. T. Zweigoff), as well as all the recent films for which he has also been picture editor.

He has also been involved in film restoration, notably Orson Welles' *Touch of Evil* (1998) and Francis Coppola's *Apocalypse Now Redux* (2001).

Screenplays on which Murch has collaborated include *THX-1138*, directed by George Lucas, and *The Black Stallion* (1979, uncredited), directed by Carroll Ballard. Murch directed and co-wrote the film *Return to Oz*, released by Disney in 1985.